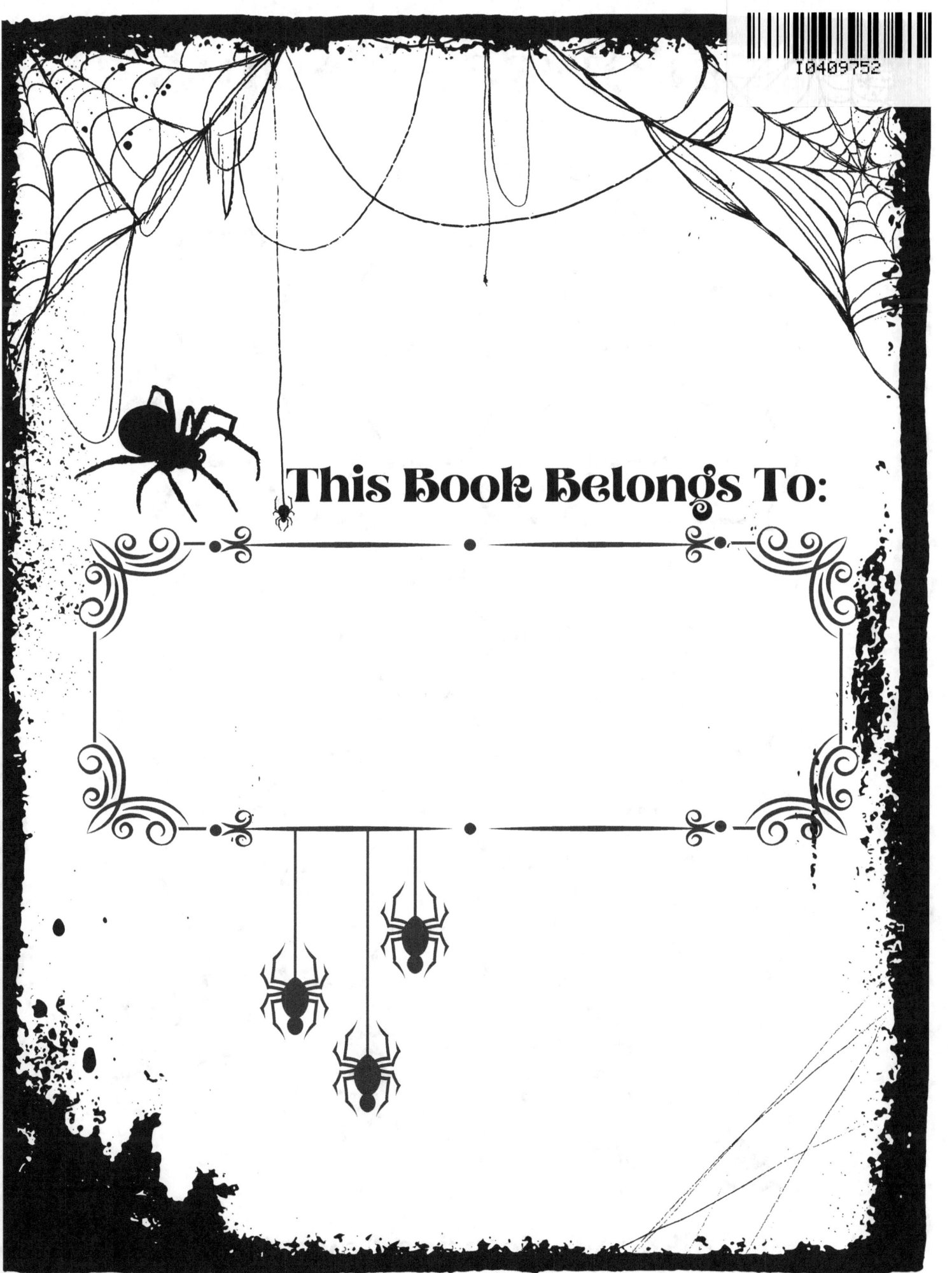

This Book Belongs To:

Halloween Haunts

Color Testing Page

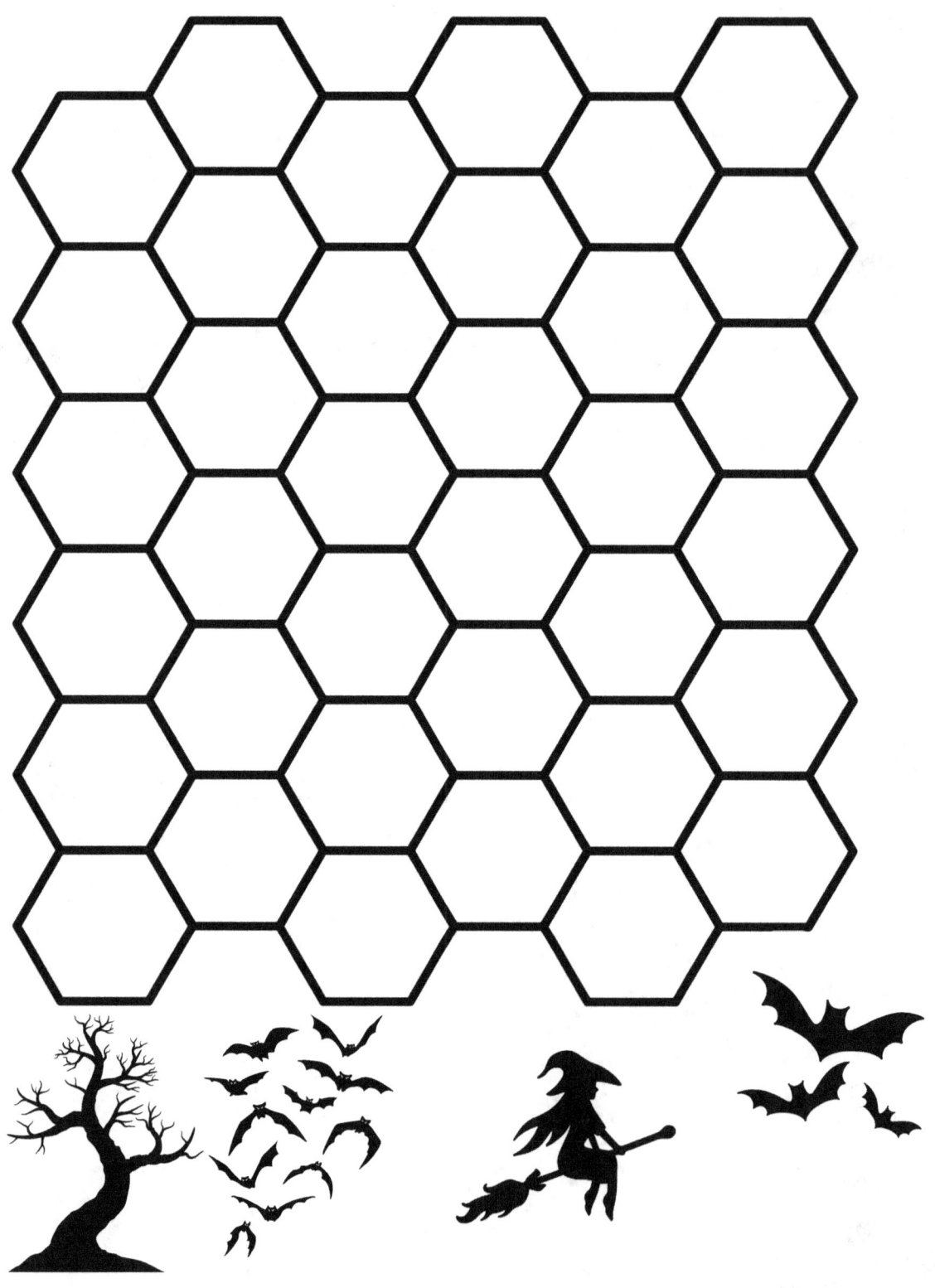

A Spooky Coloring Adventure

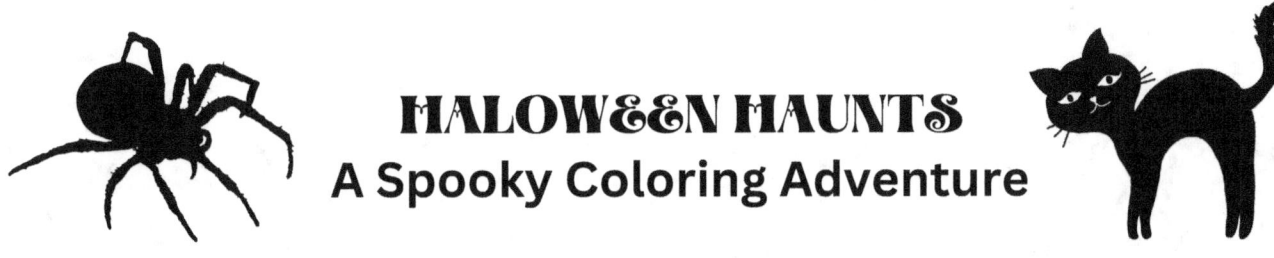

HALOWEEN HAUNTS
A Spooky Coloring Adventure

"Step into the enchanting world of Halloween with "Halloween Haunts: A Spooky Coloring Adventure." This 82-page adult coloring book is a celebration of all things eerie, whimsical, and mysterious. Each page invites you to immerse yourself in the bewitching town of Ravenbrook, renowned for its legendary Halloween celebrations. Inside, you'll find intricately detailed illustrations that capture the essence of this magical season. From the grand Haunted Mansion draped in ivy and cobwebs to the moonlit Enchanted Forest where fairies dance among twisted trees, every page offers a new enchantment to color.

Join the masked revelers at the elegant Masquerade Ball, where ghosts and ghouls waltz alongside the living. Explore the sprawling pumpkin patch guarded by a mischievous scarecrow, and witness the Witch of Ravenbrook brew her mystical potions in her lair filled with spell books and herbs.

As you turn the pages of "Halloween Haunts," let your creativity run wild. Immerse yourself in the whimsy, spookiness, and magic of Halloween as you bring Ravenbrook to life with your colors. Whether you're a seasoned coloring enthusiast or a newcomer to the craft, this coloring book promises an enchanting and captivating experience that celebrates the spirit of Halloween like never before.

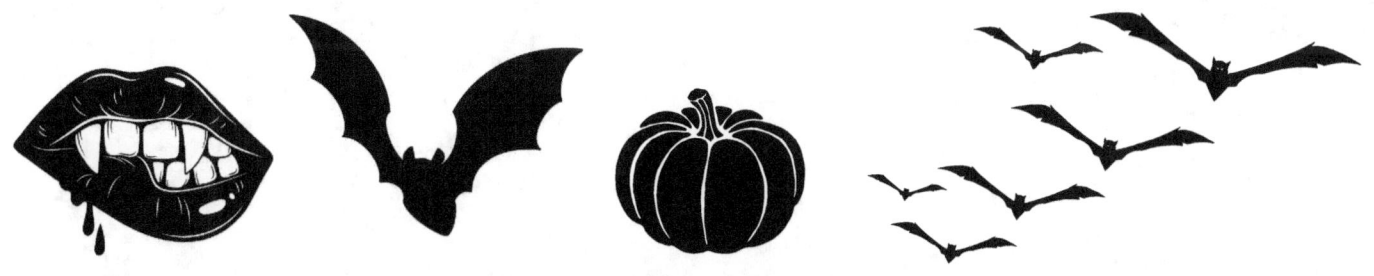

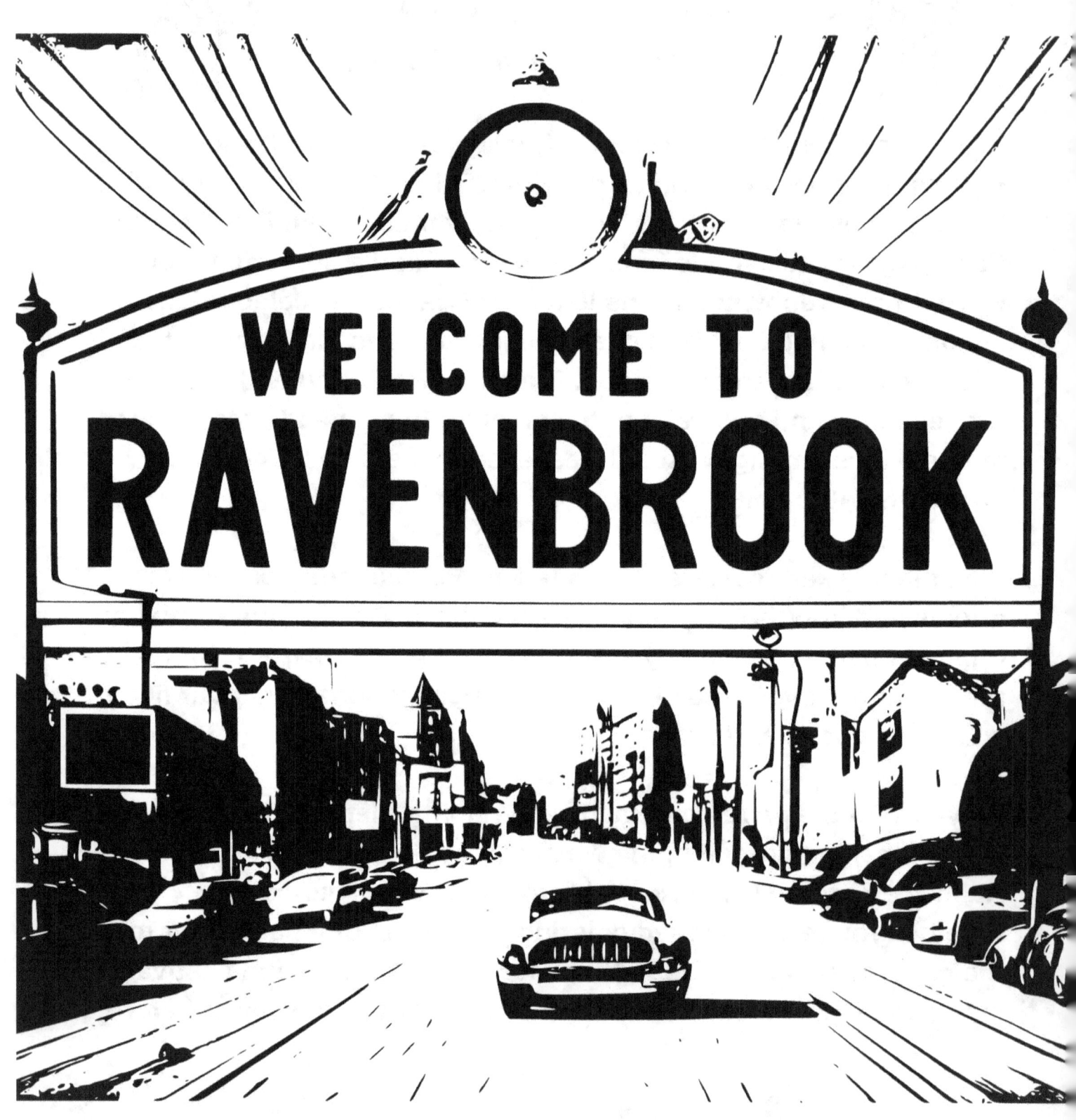

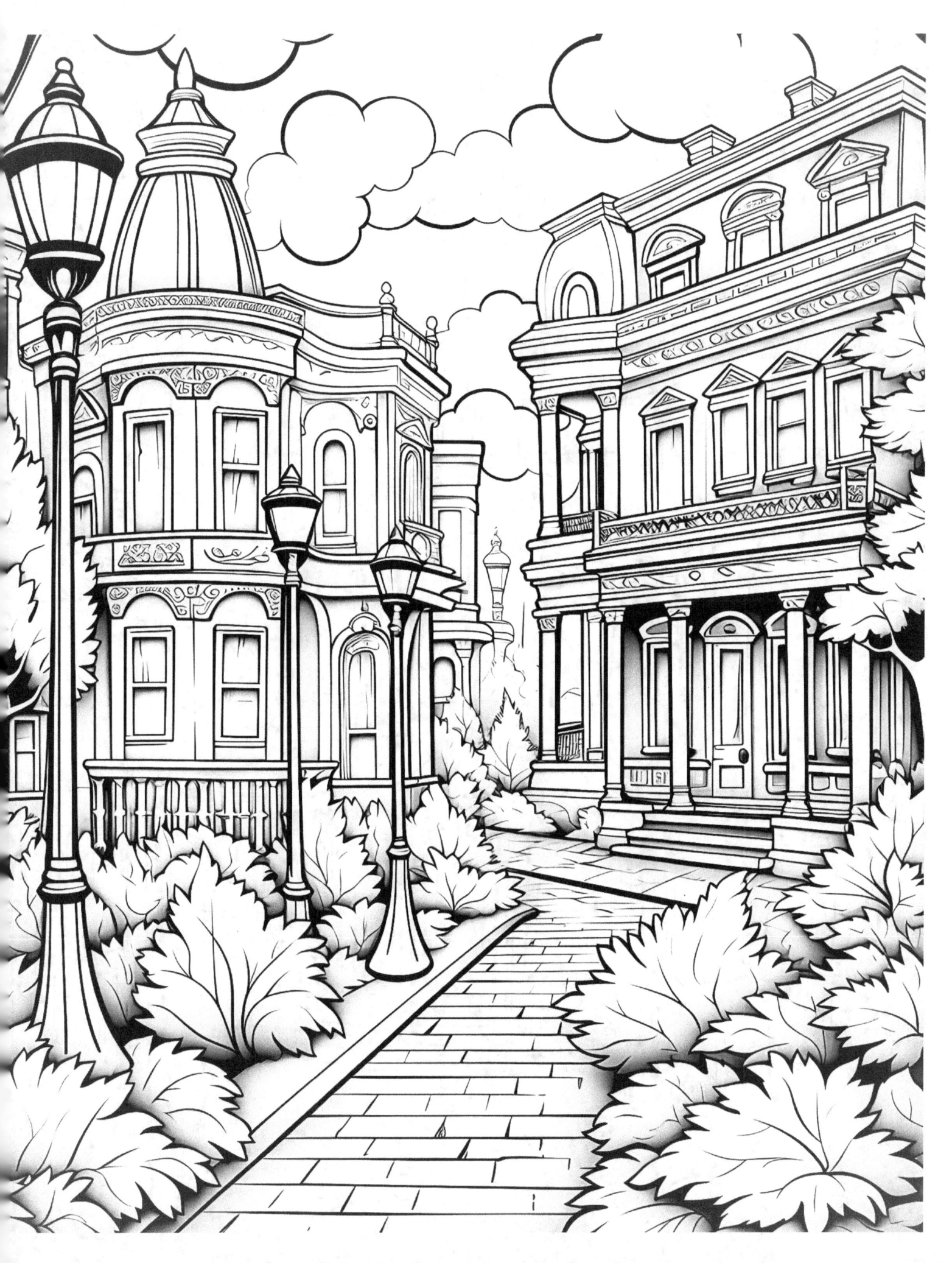

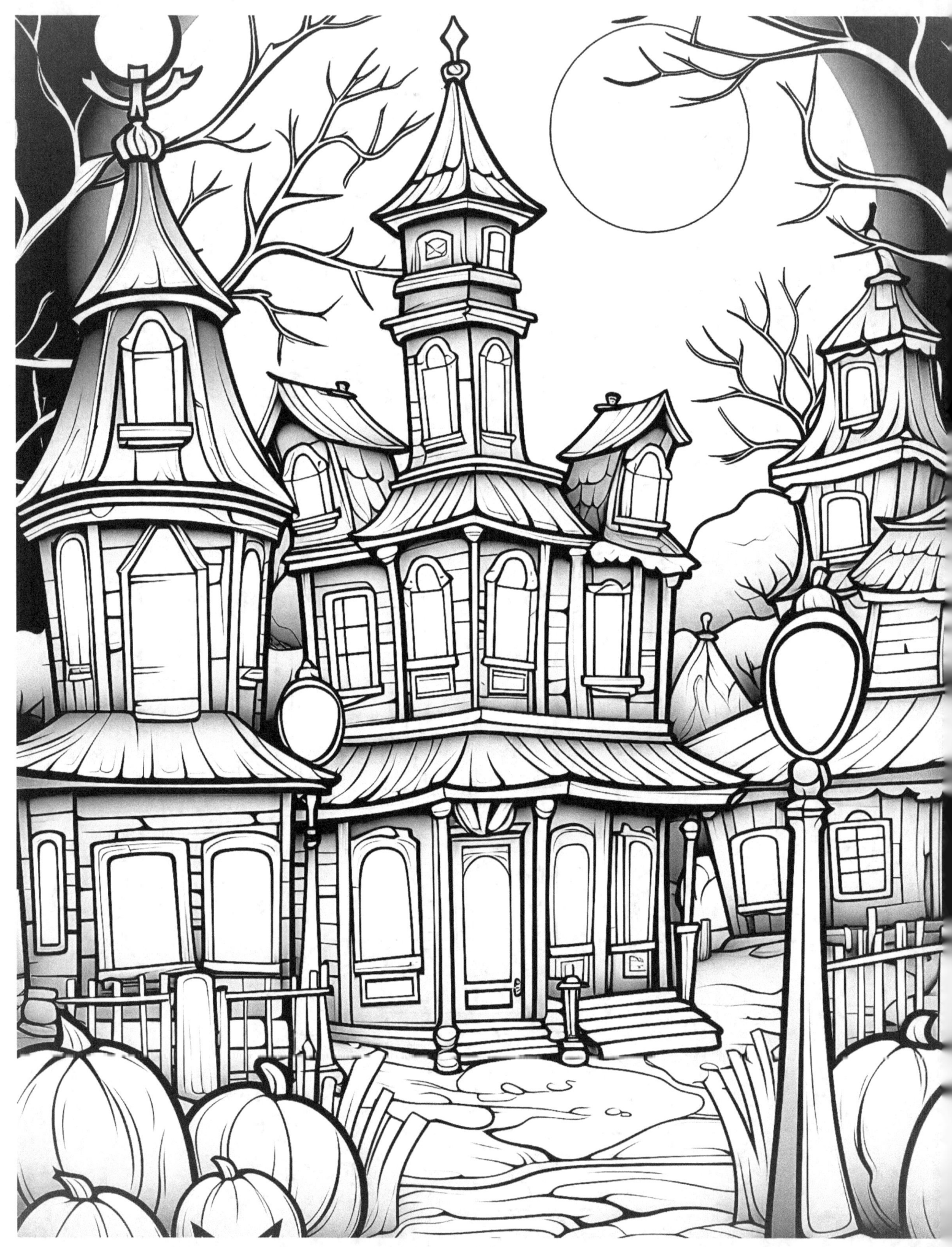

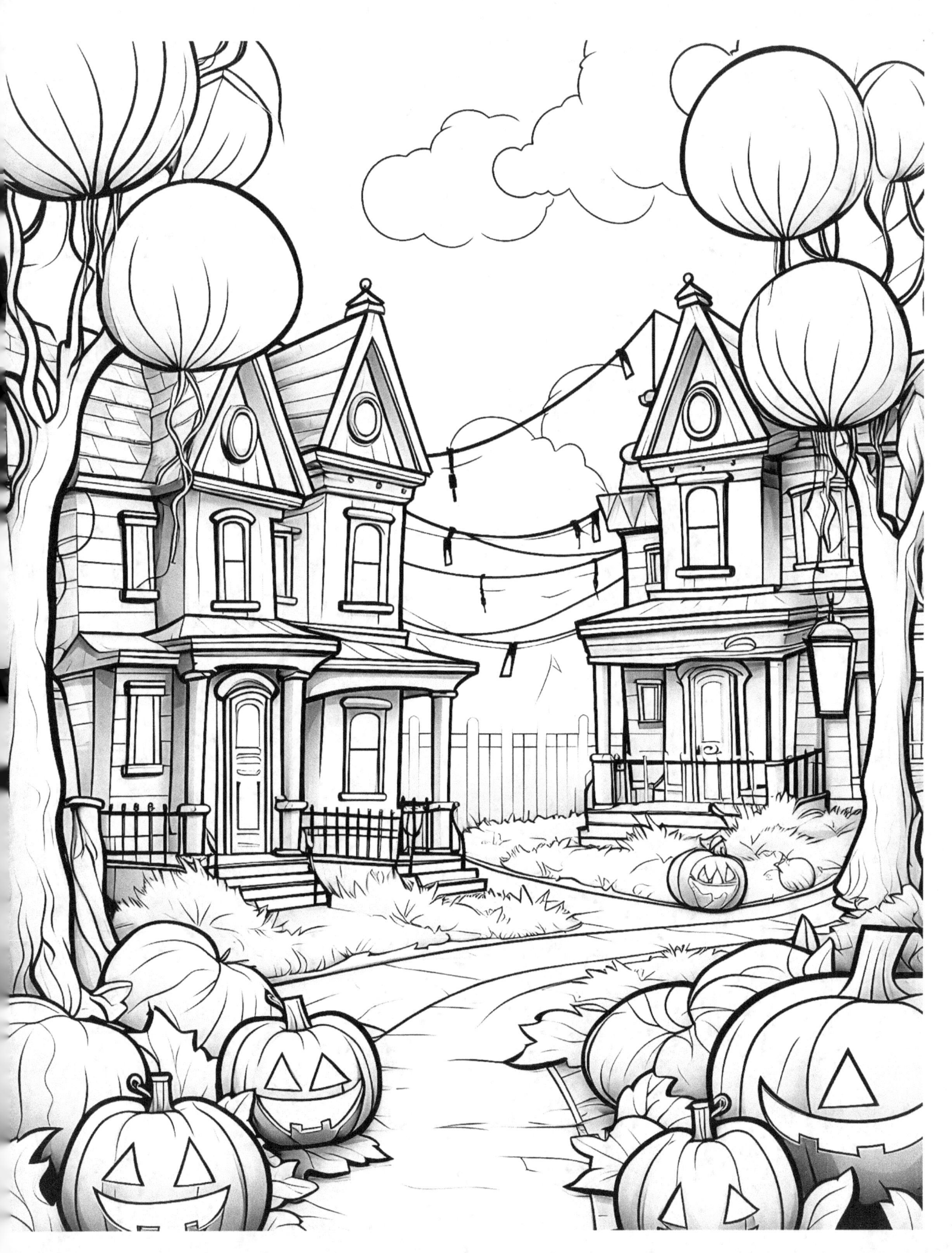

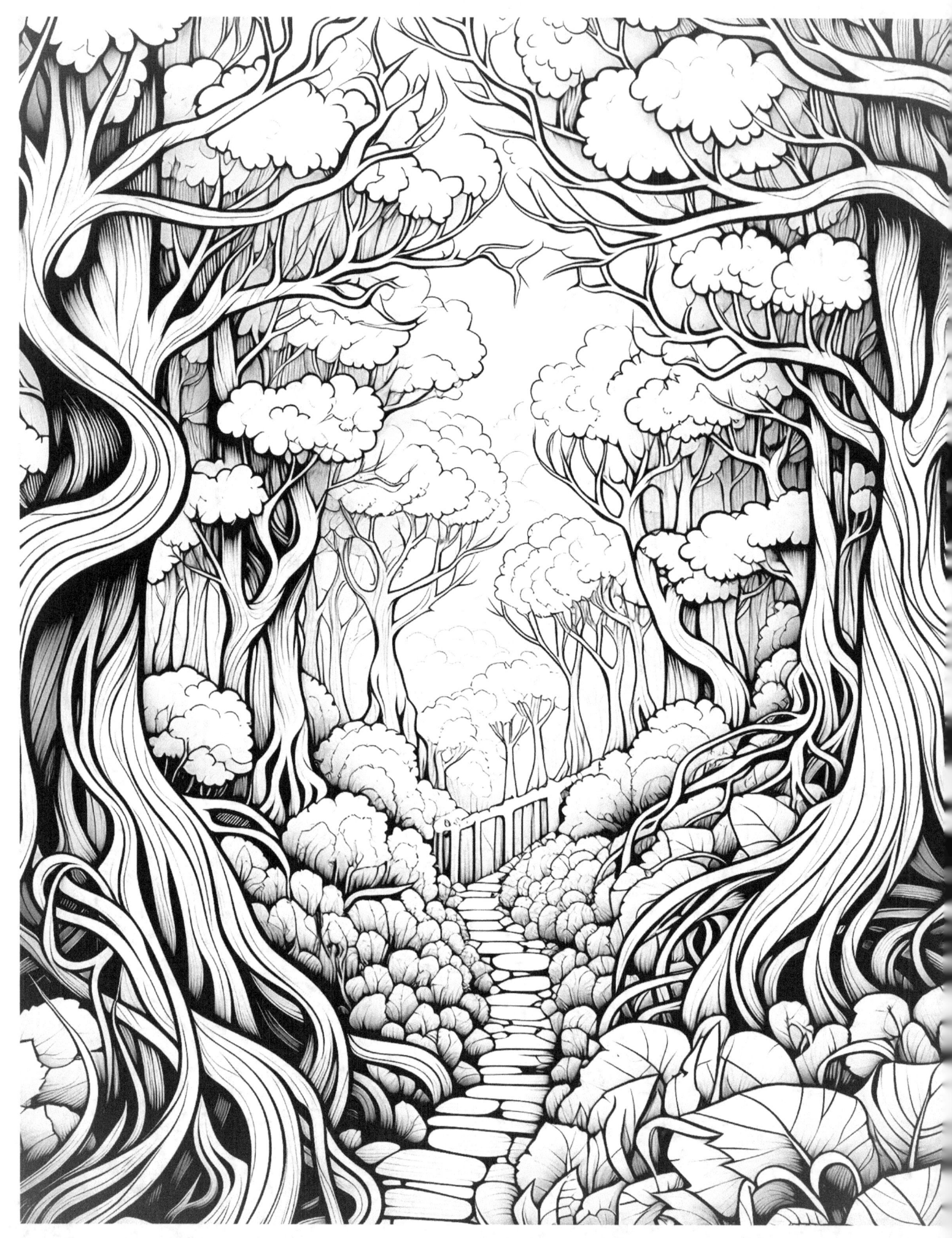

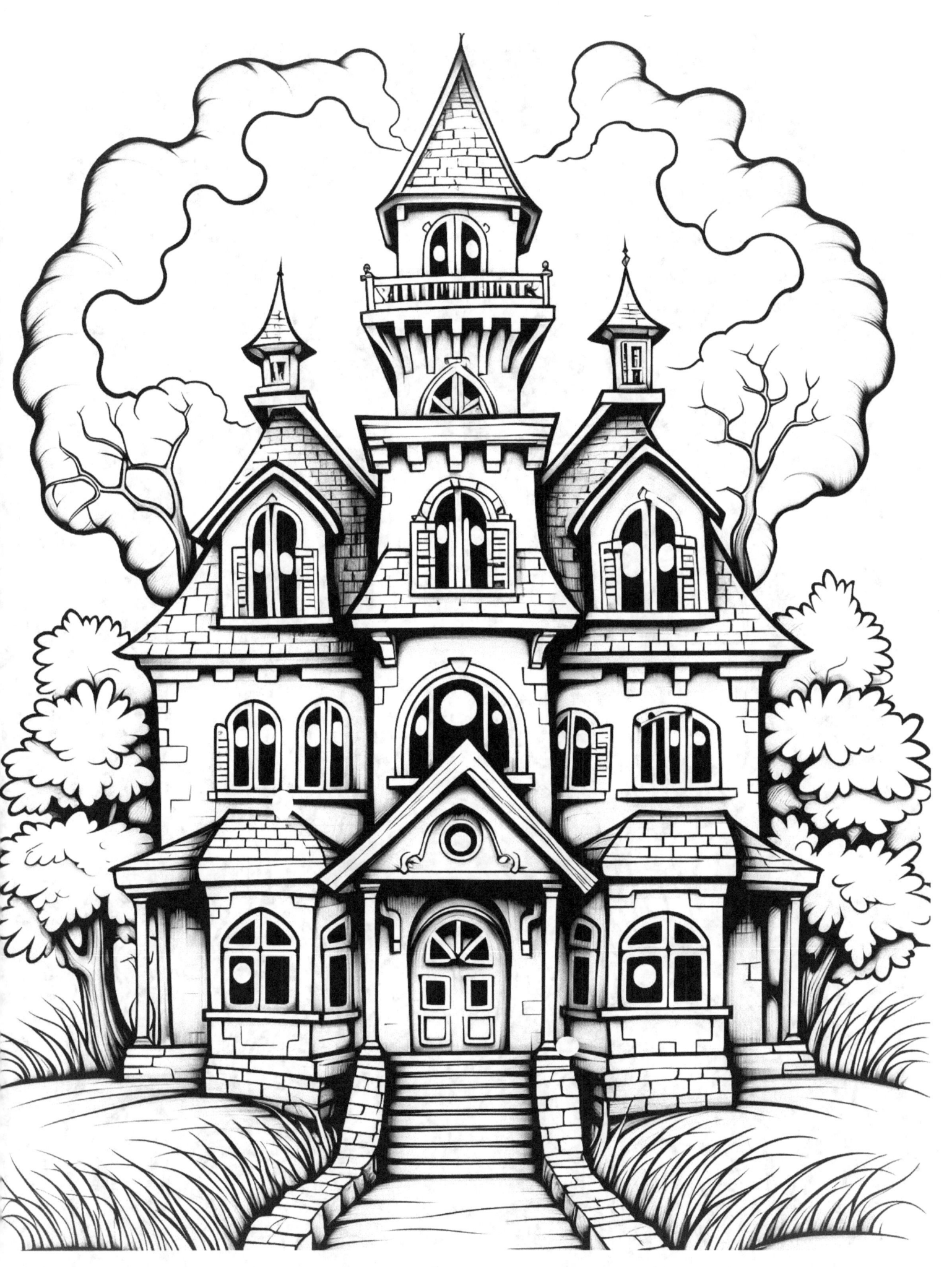

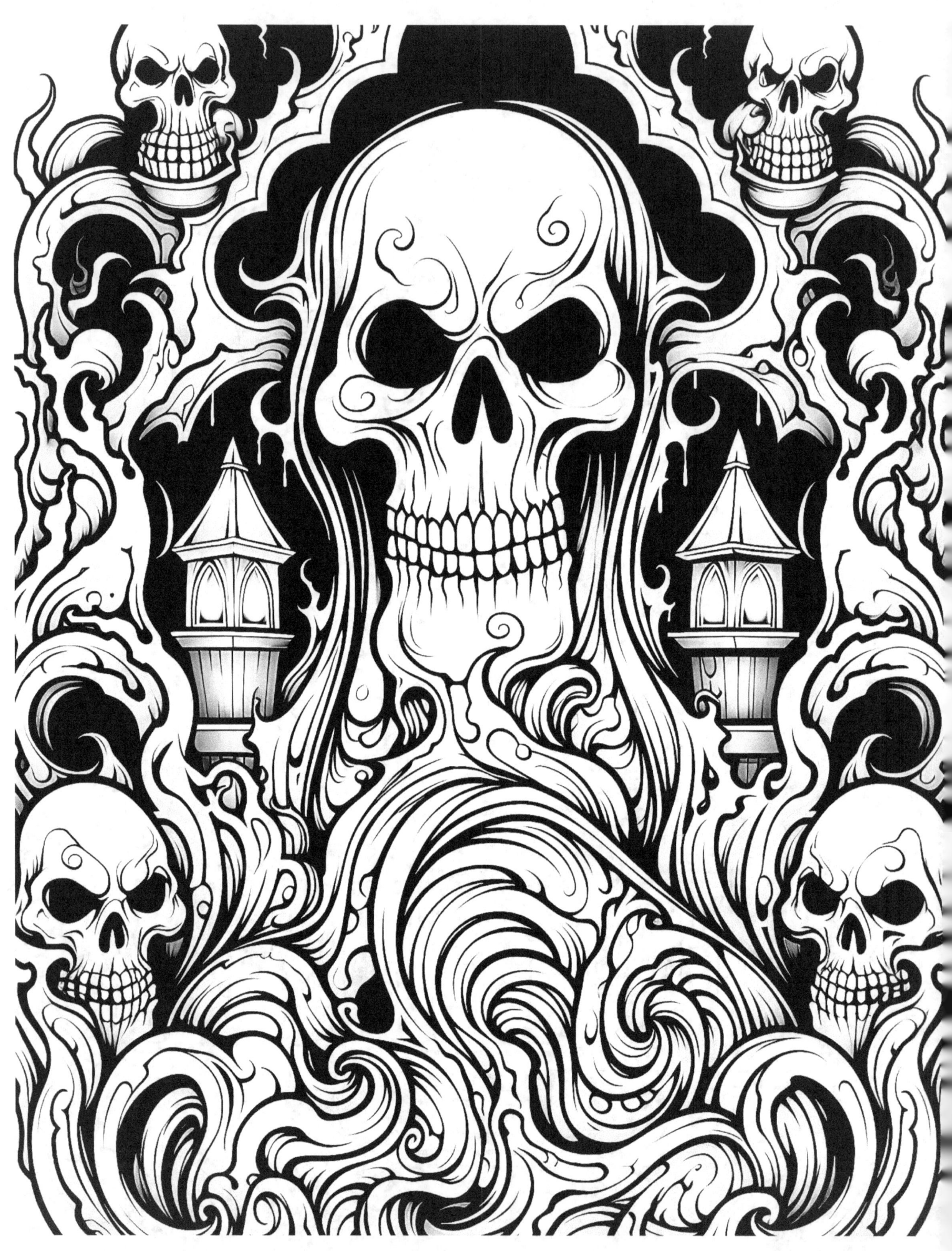

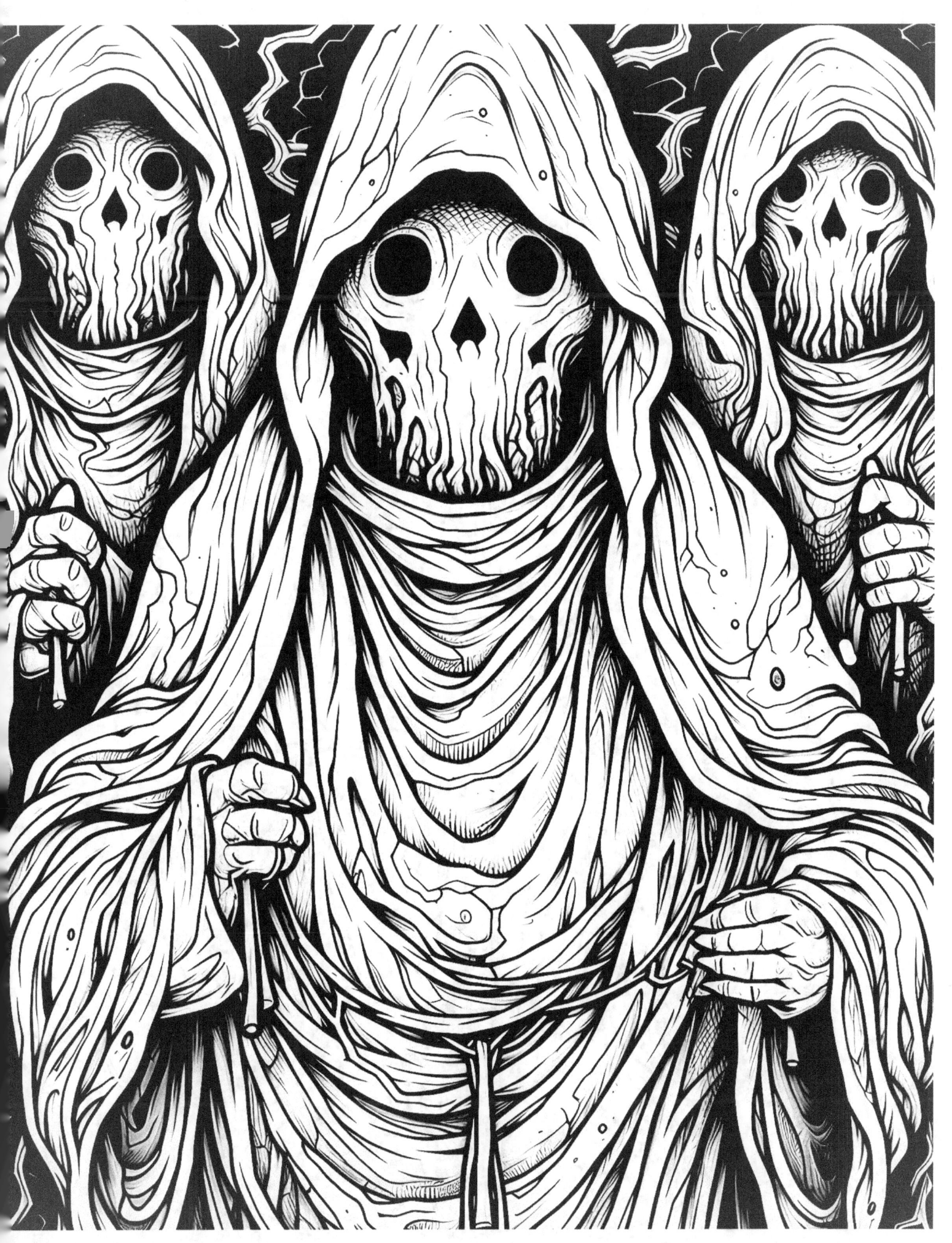

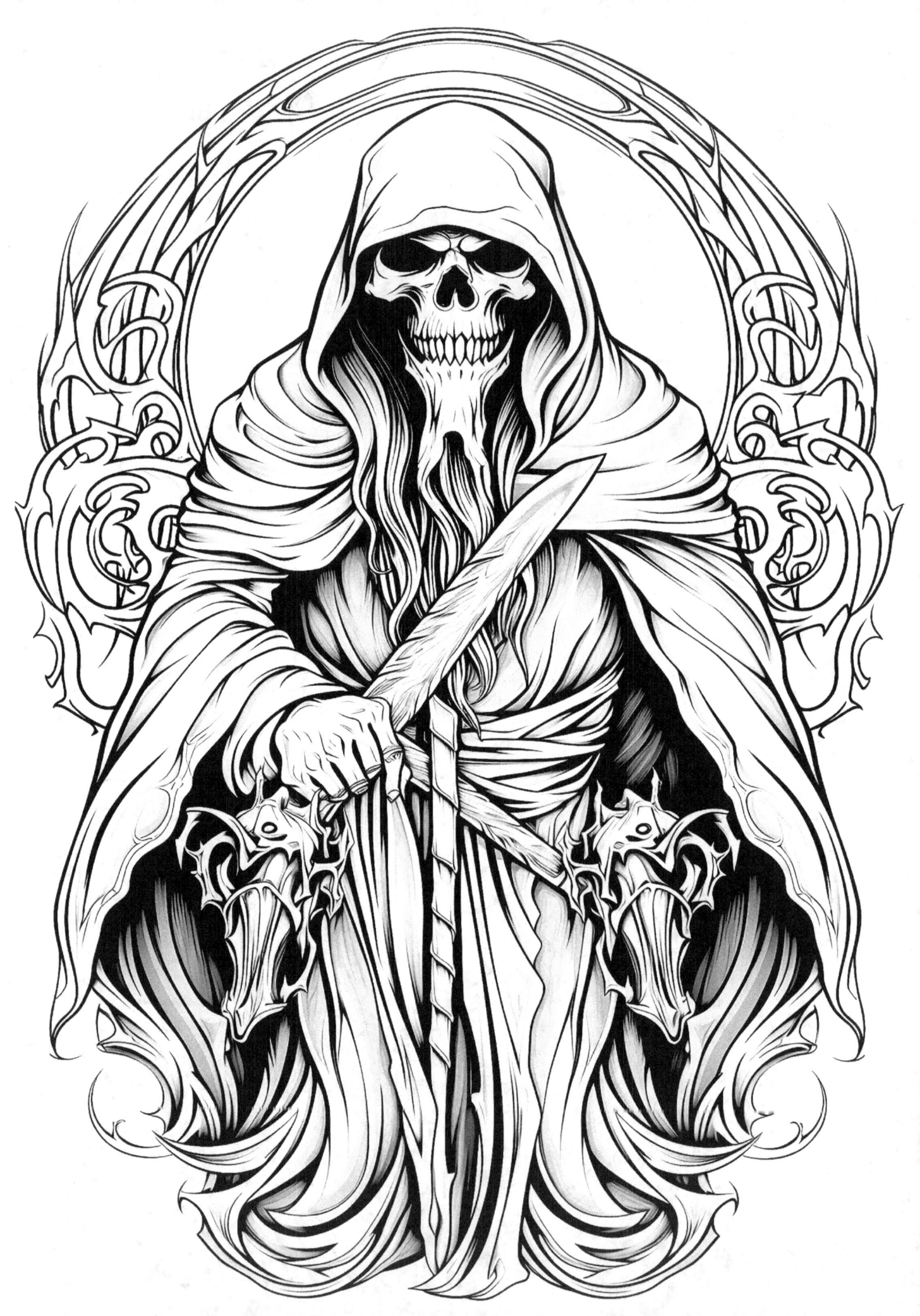

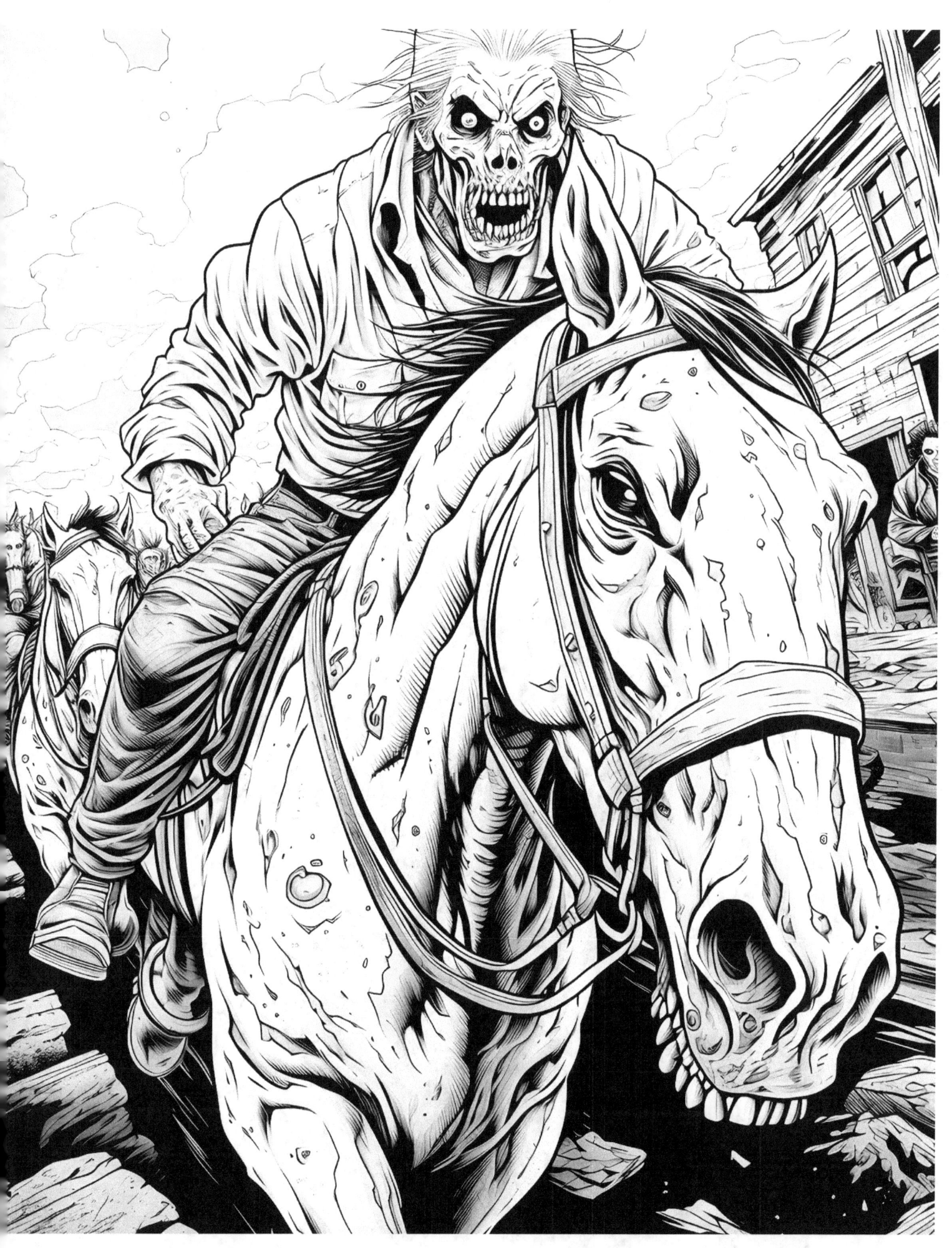

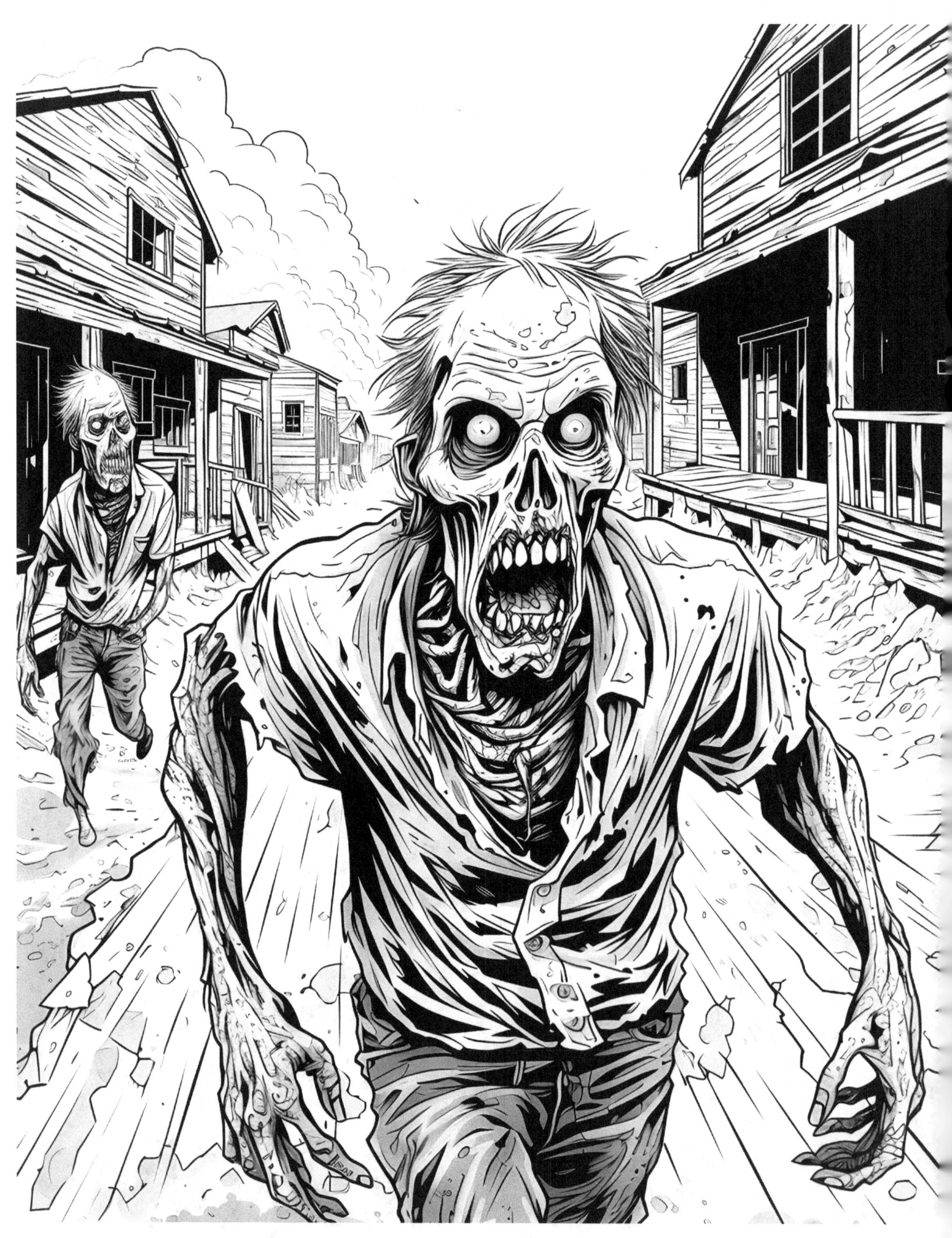

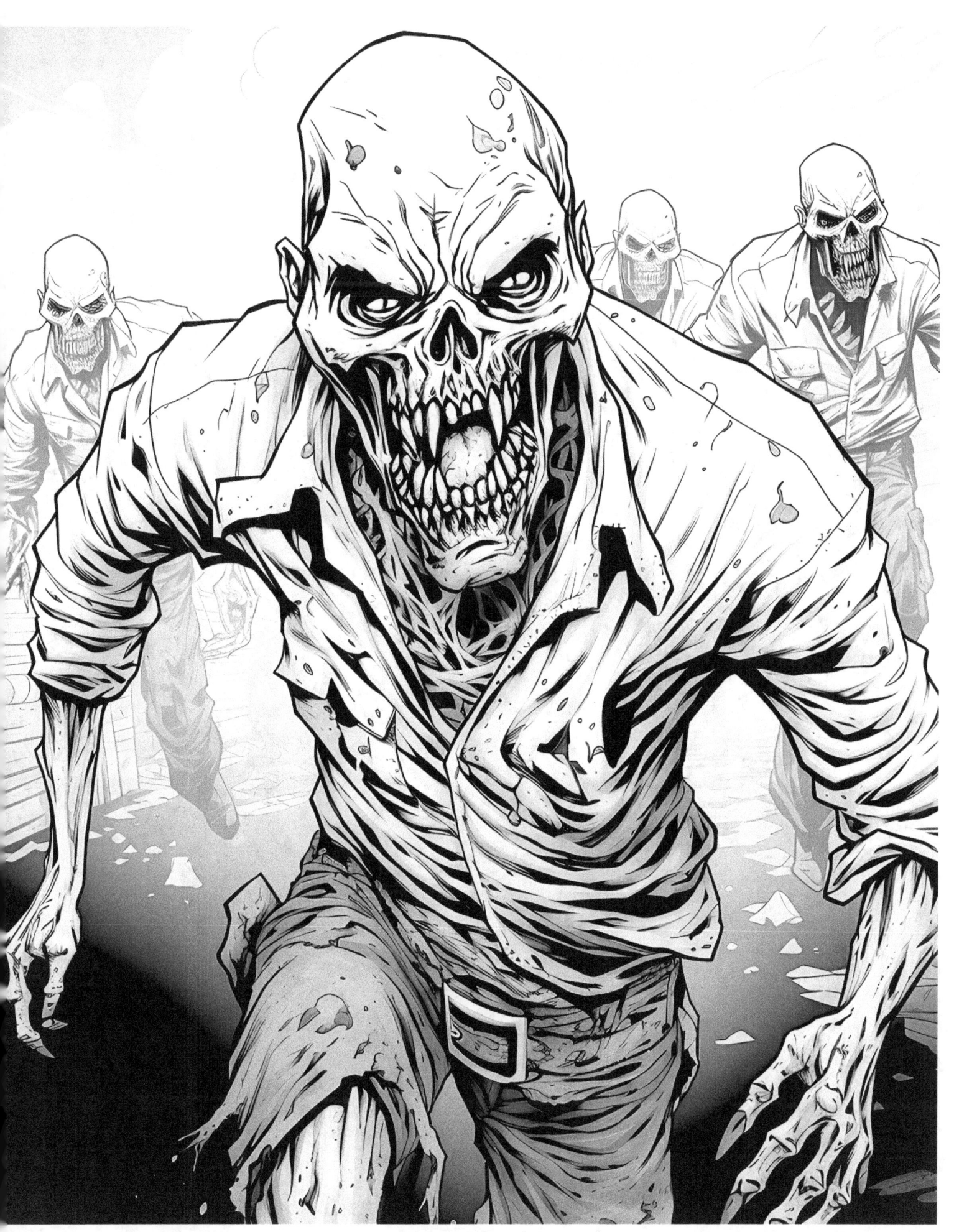

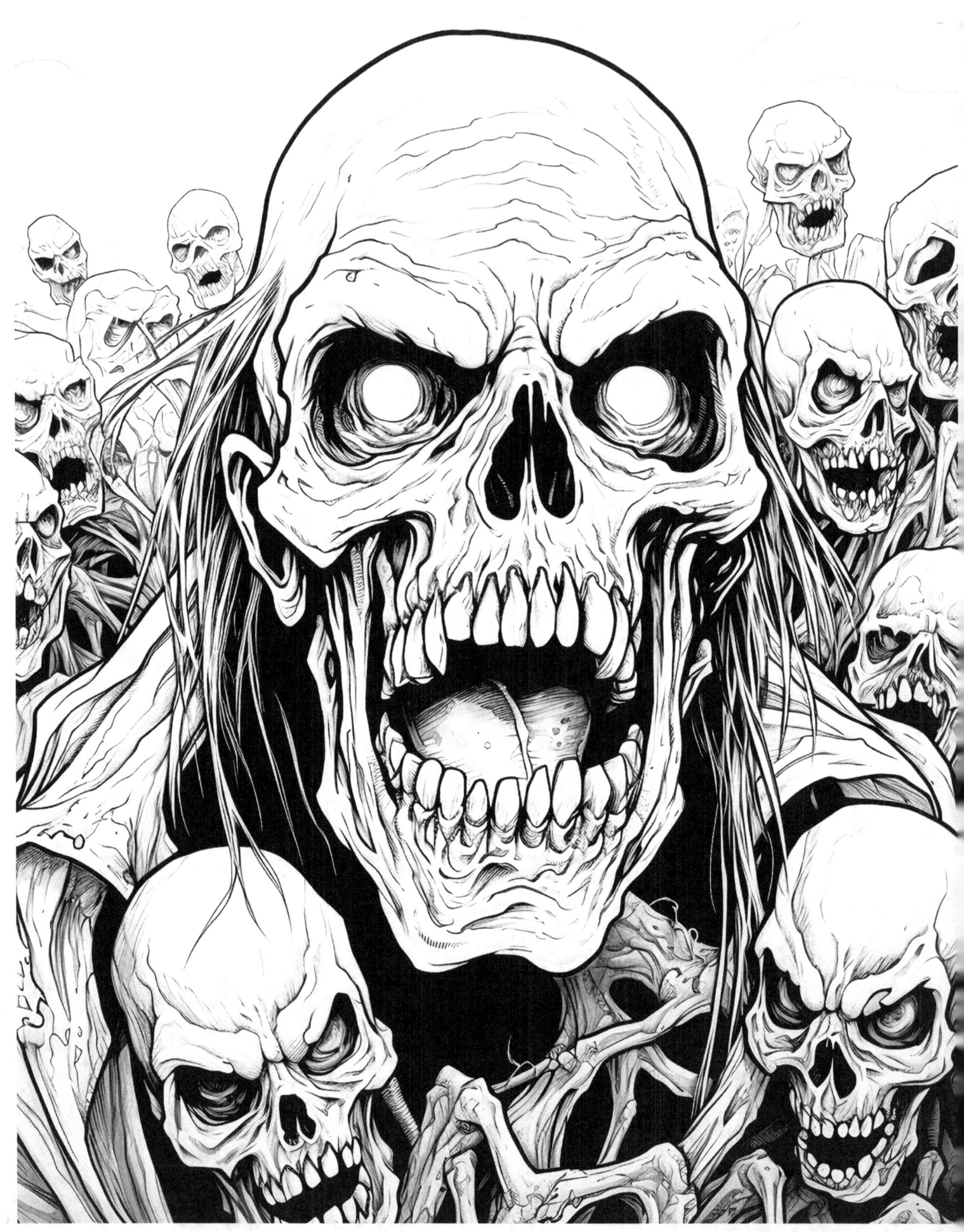

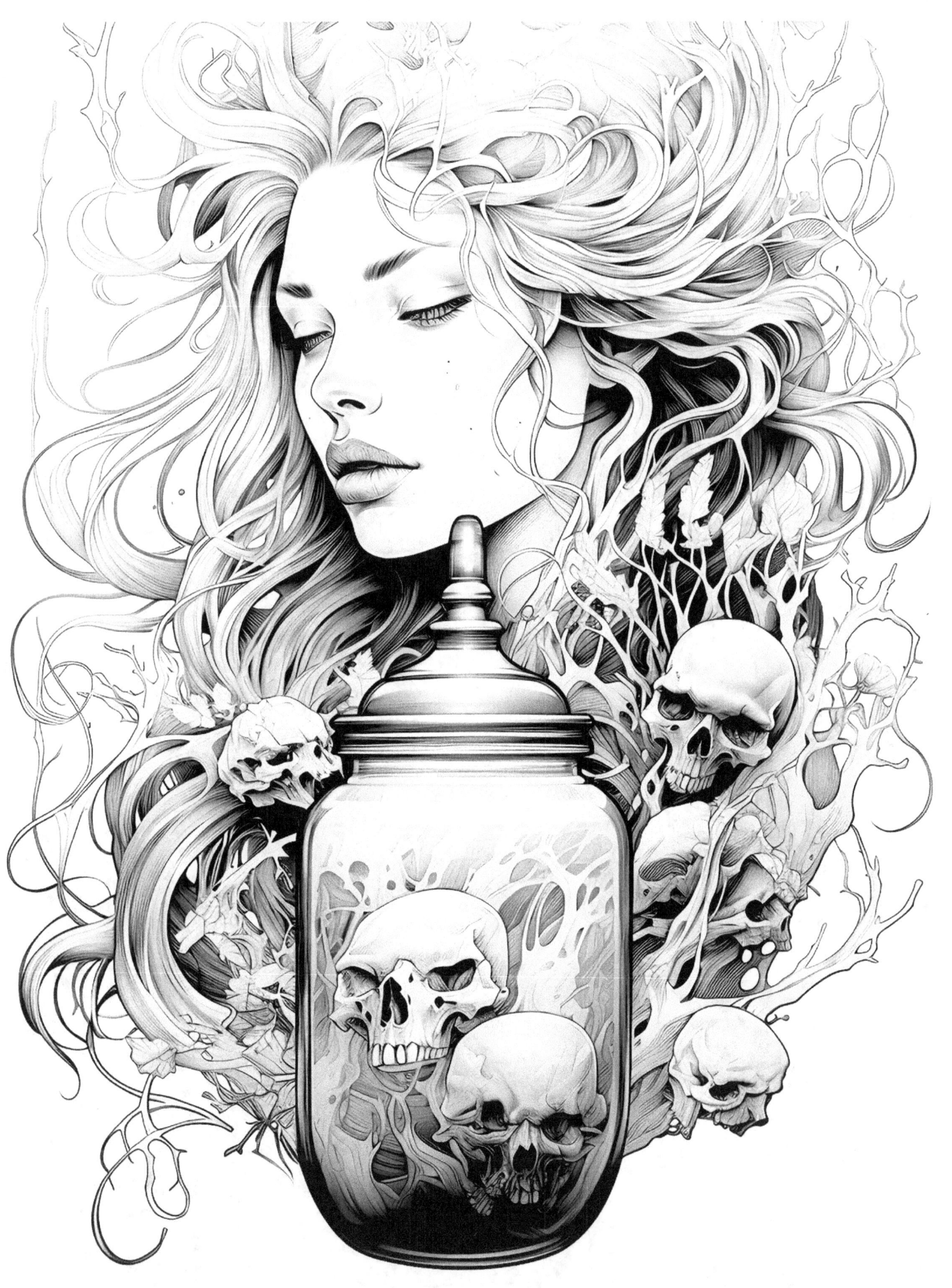

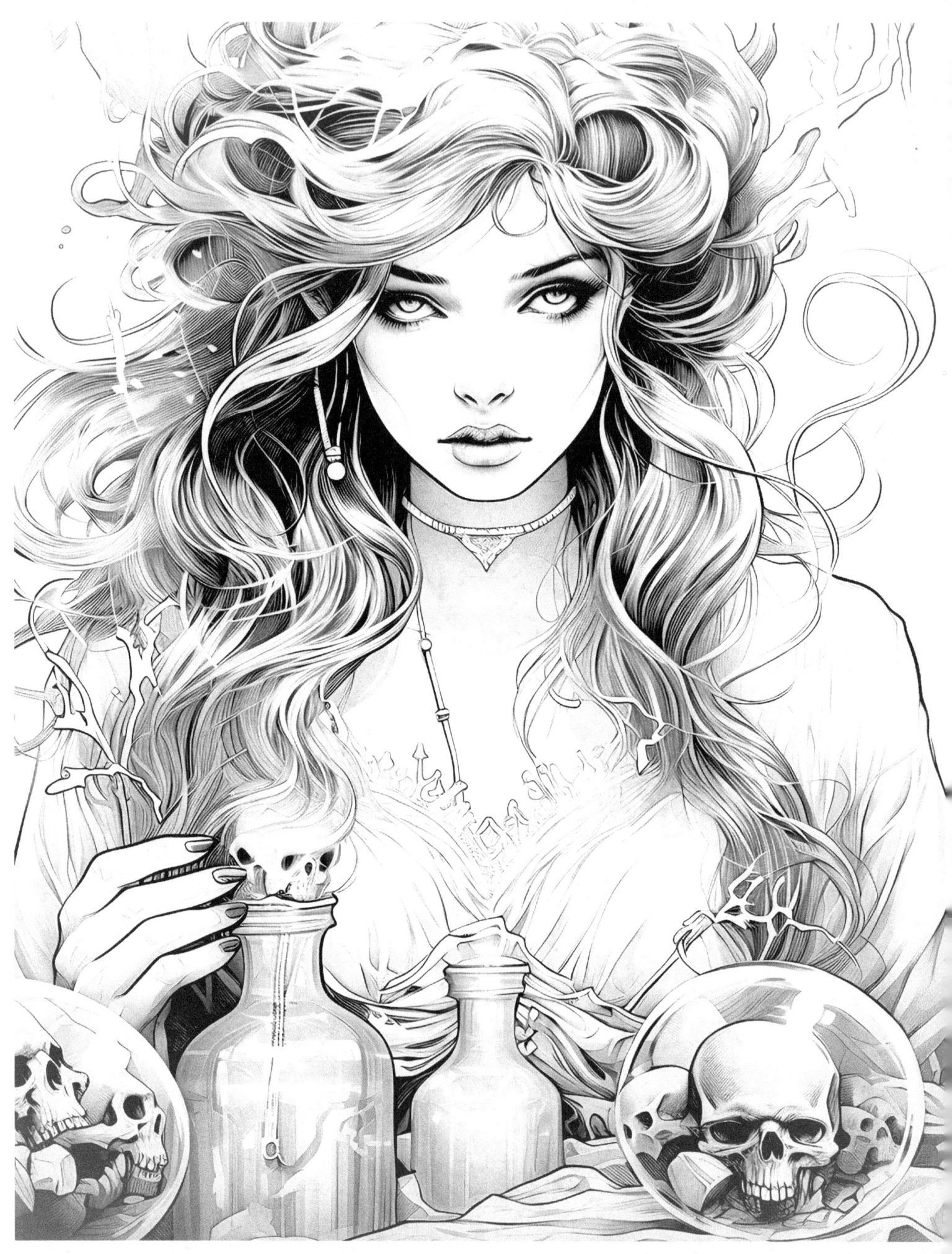

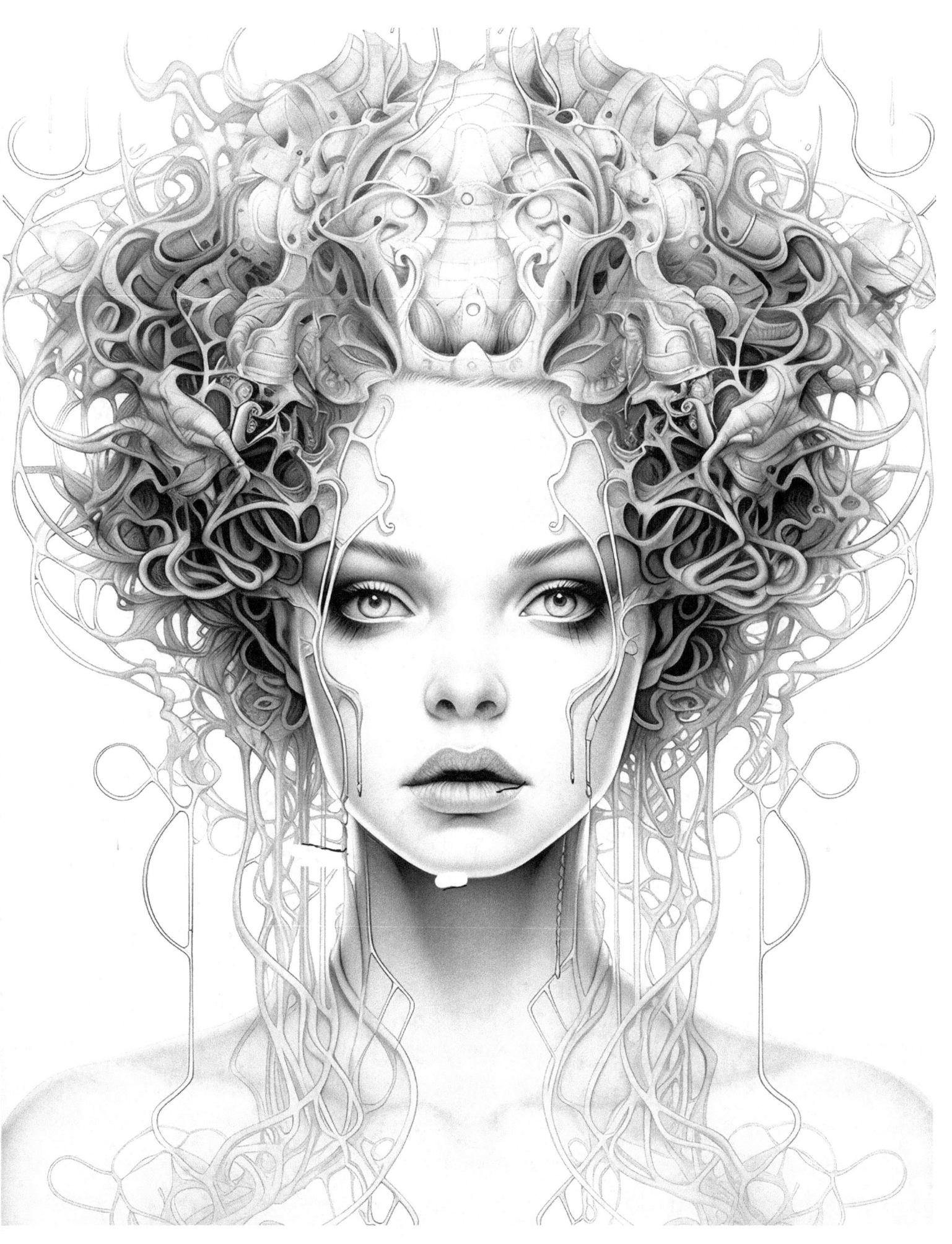

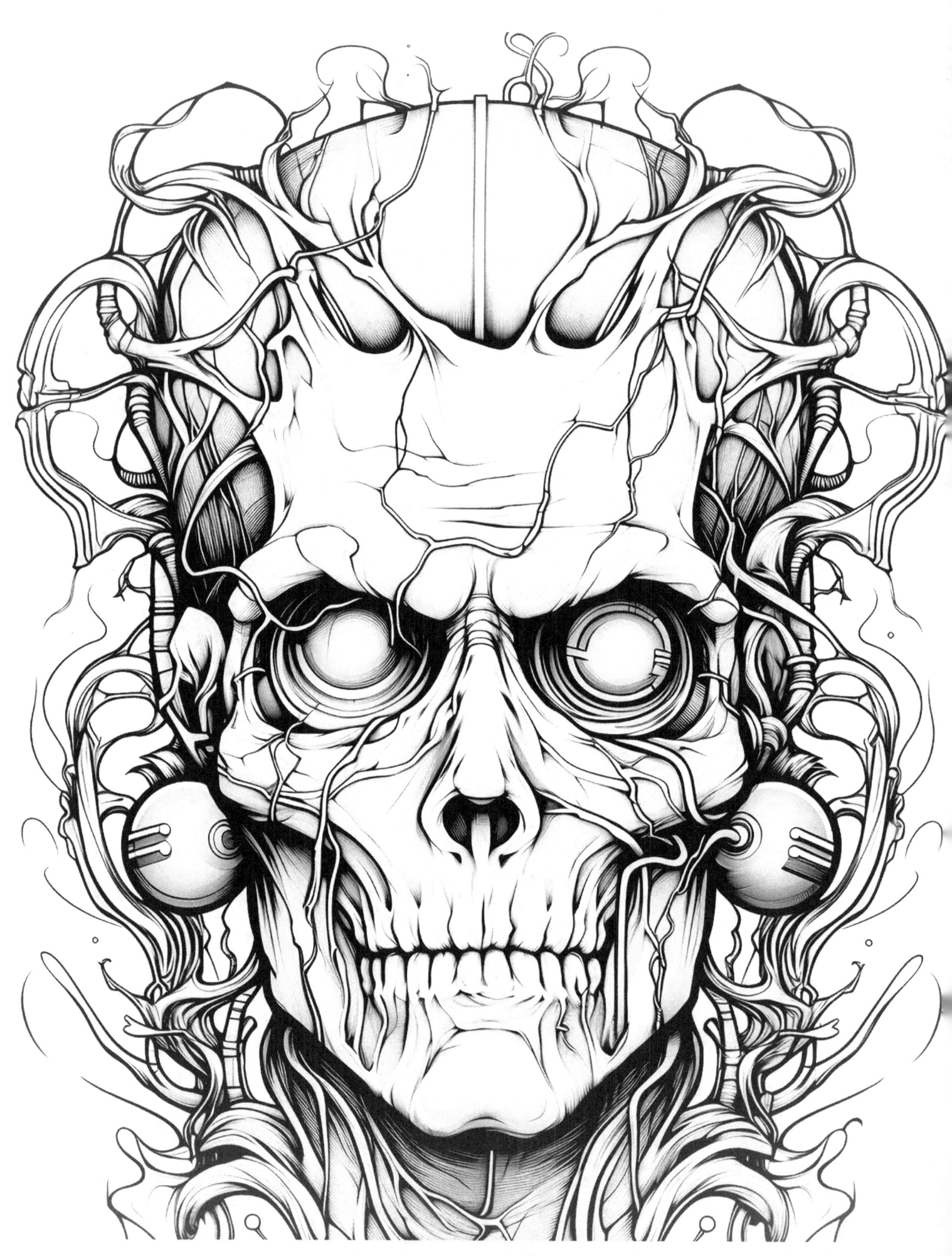

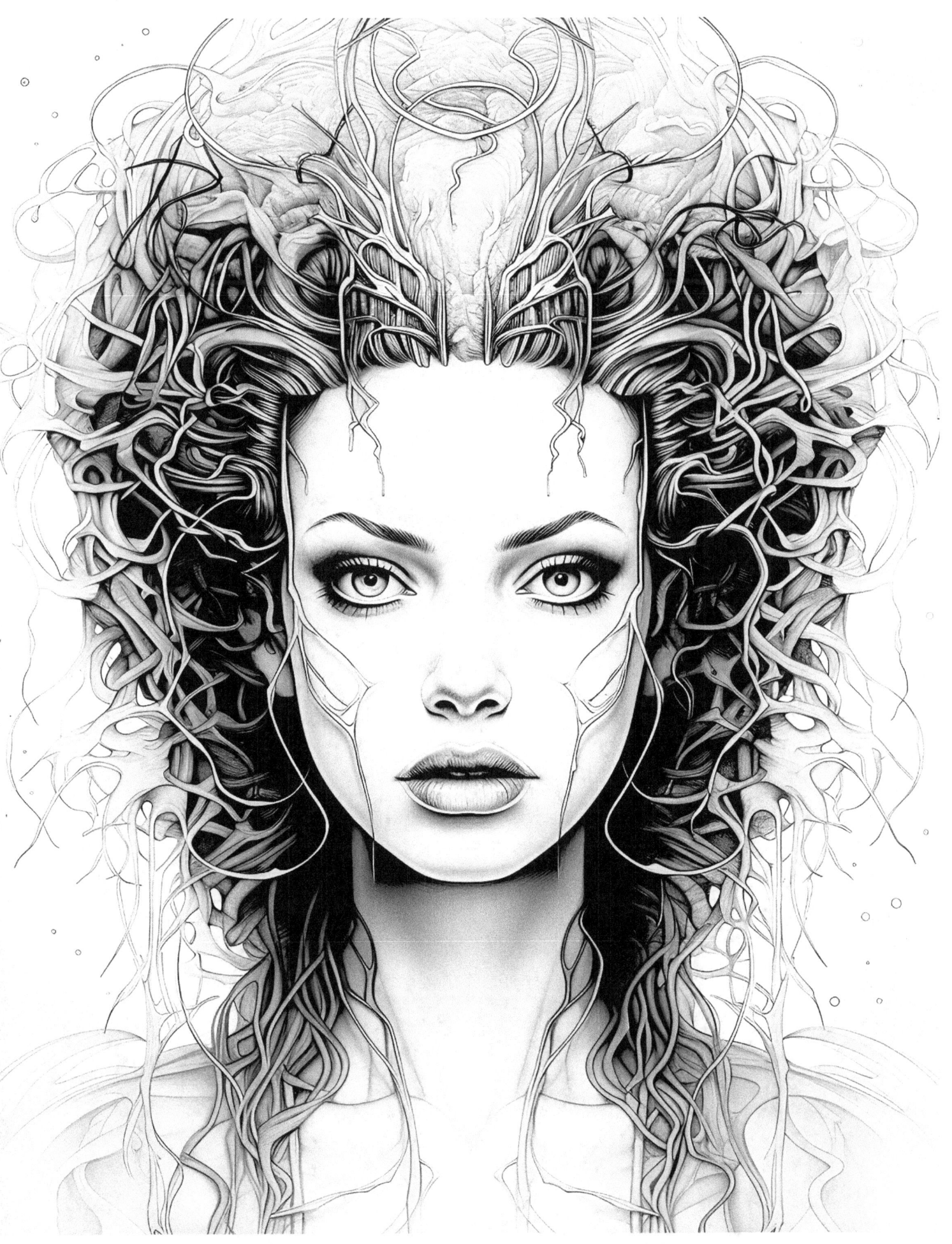

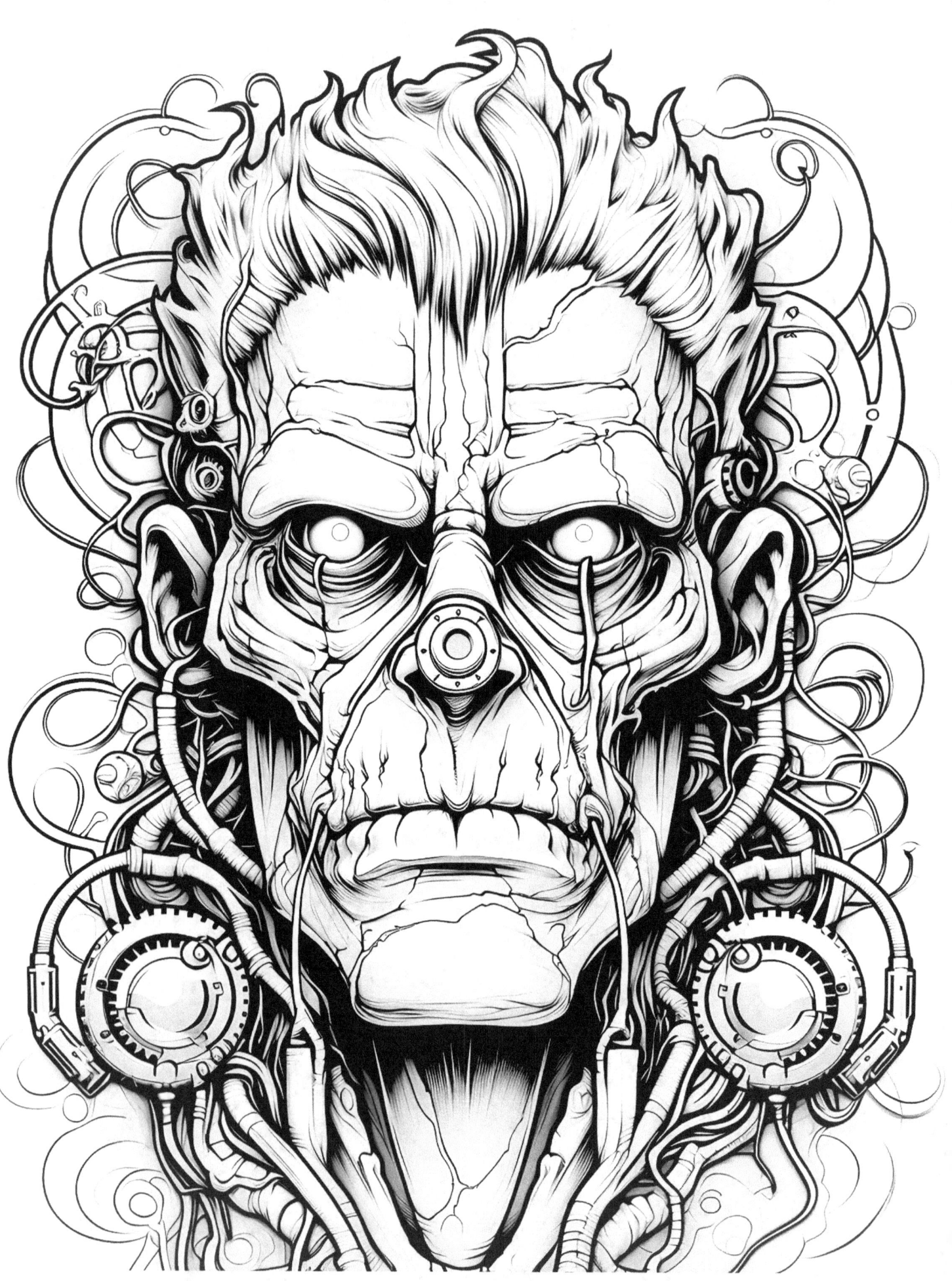

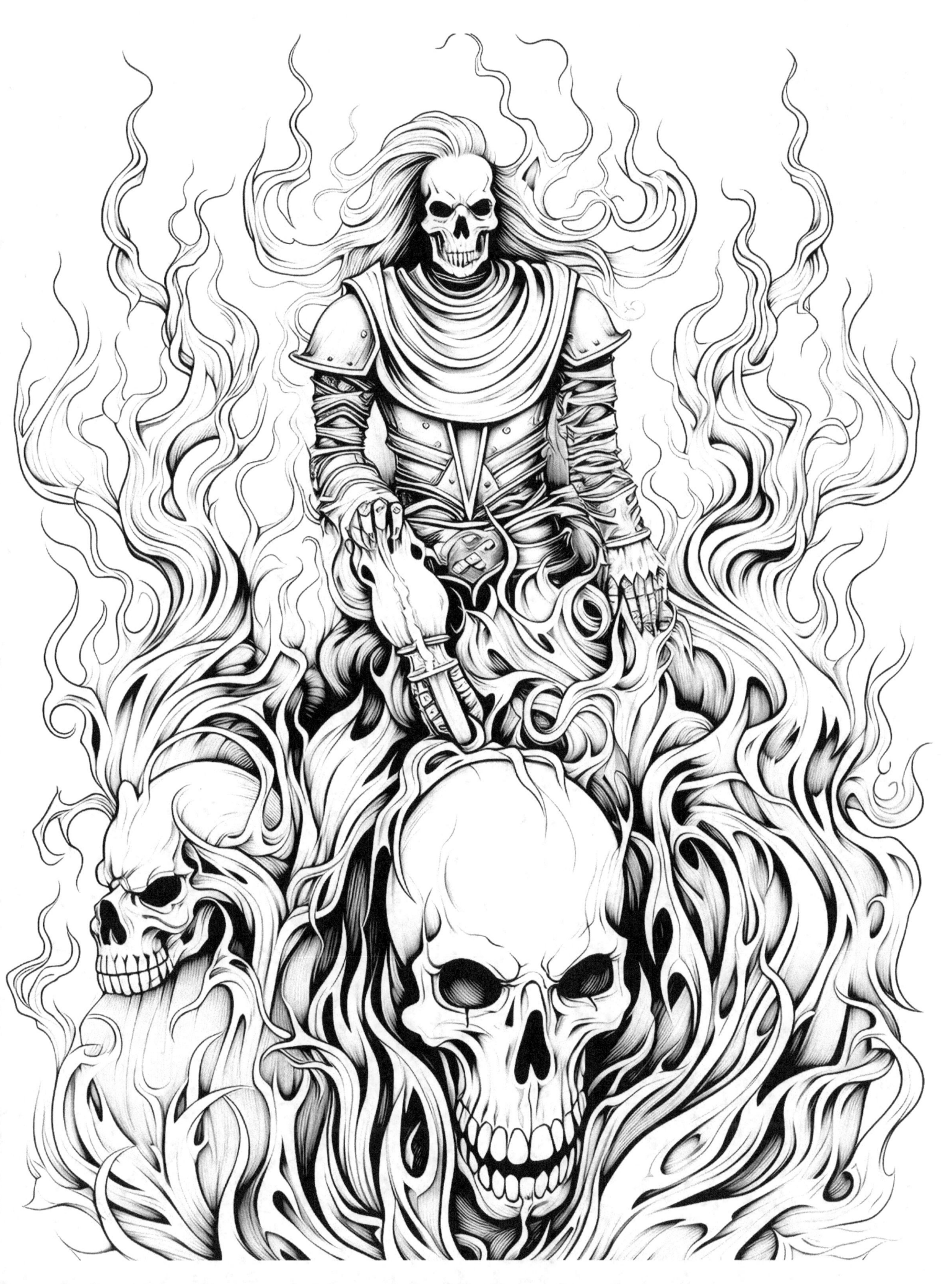

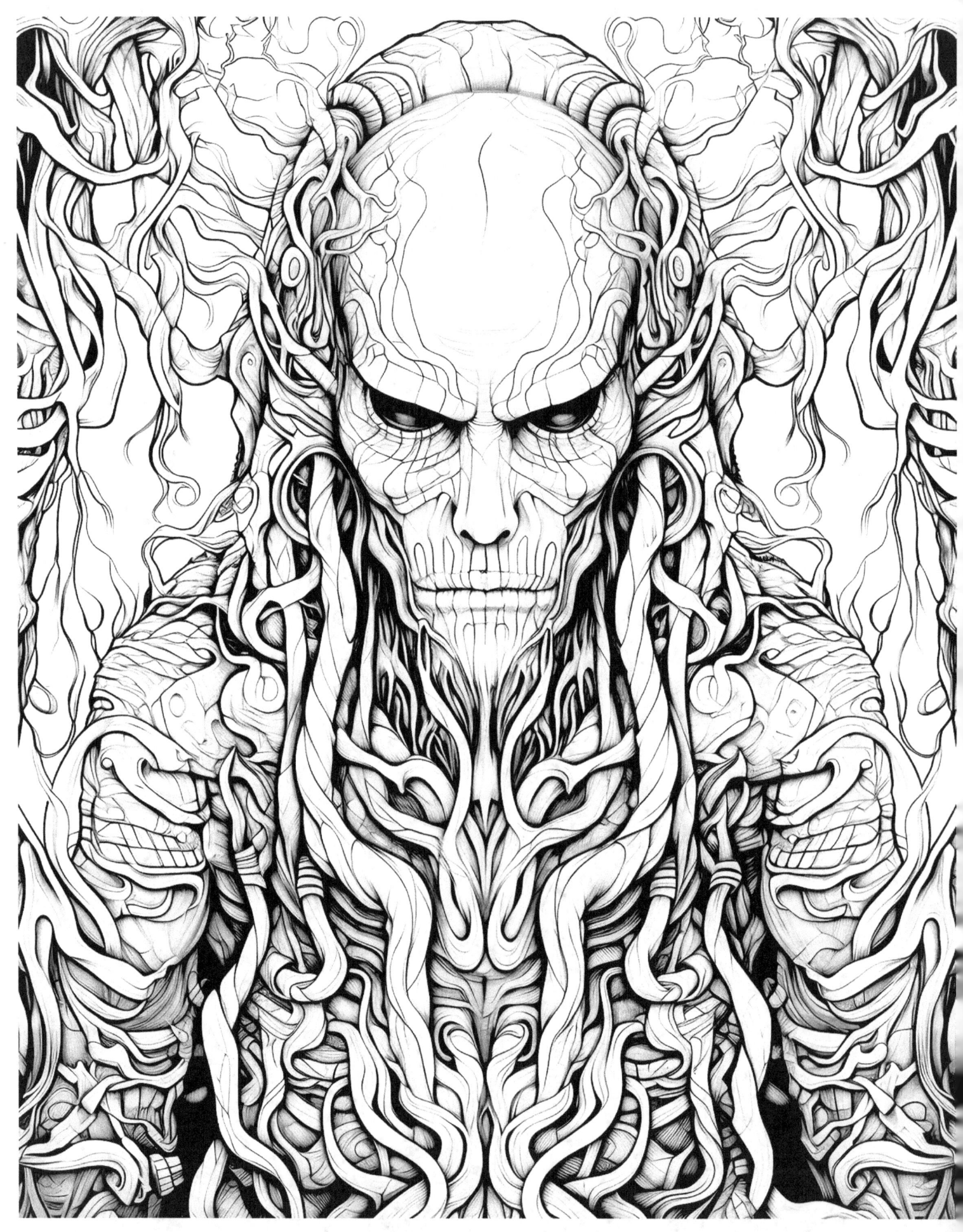

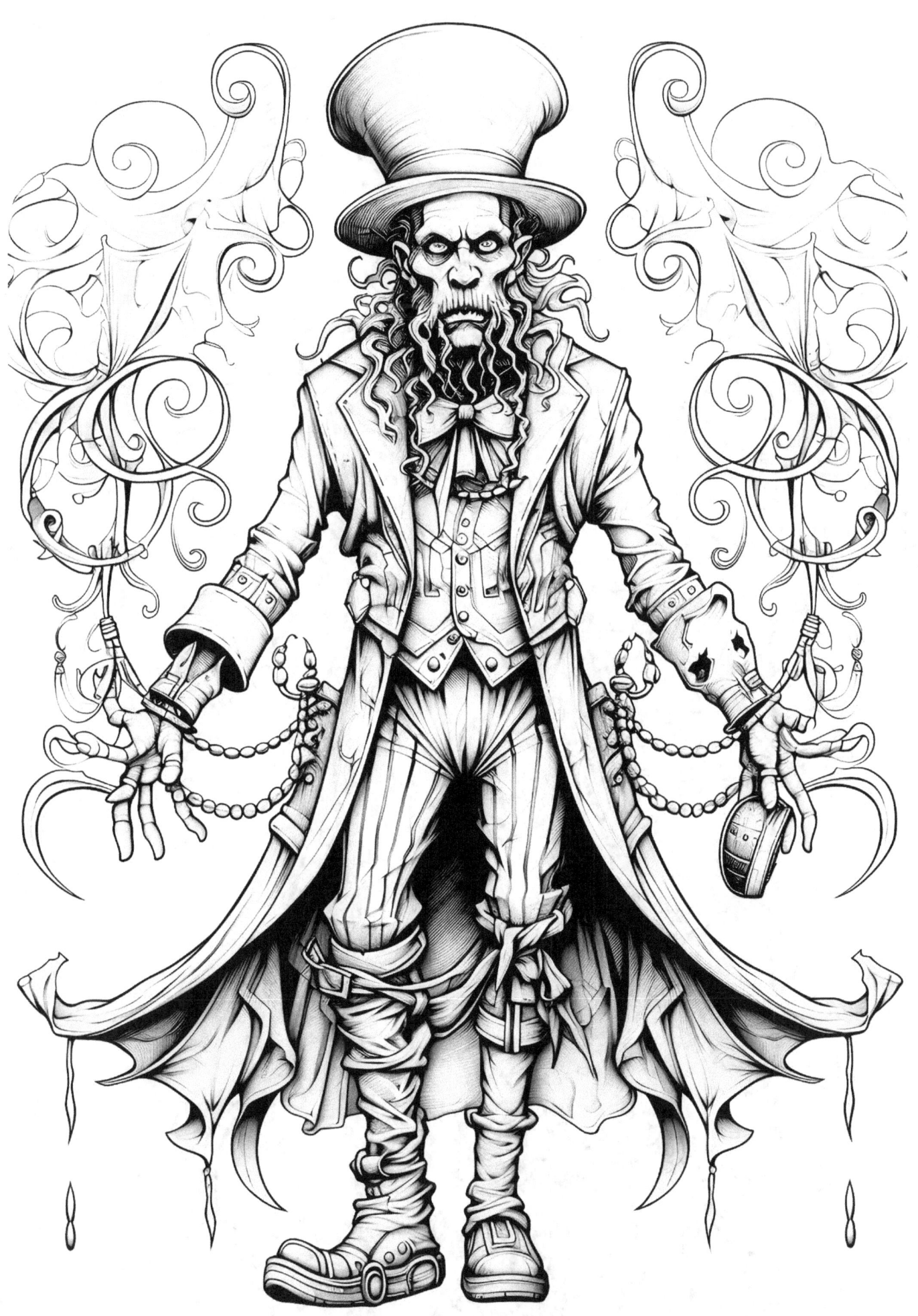

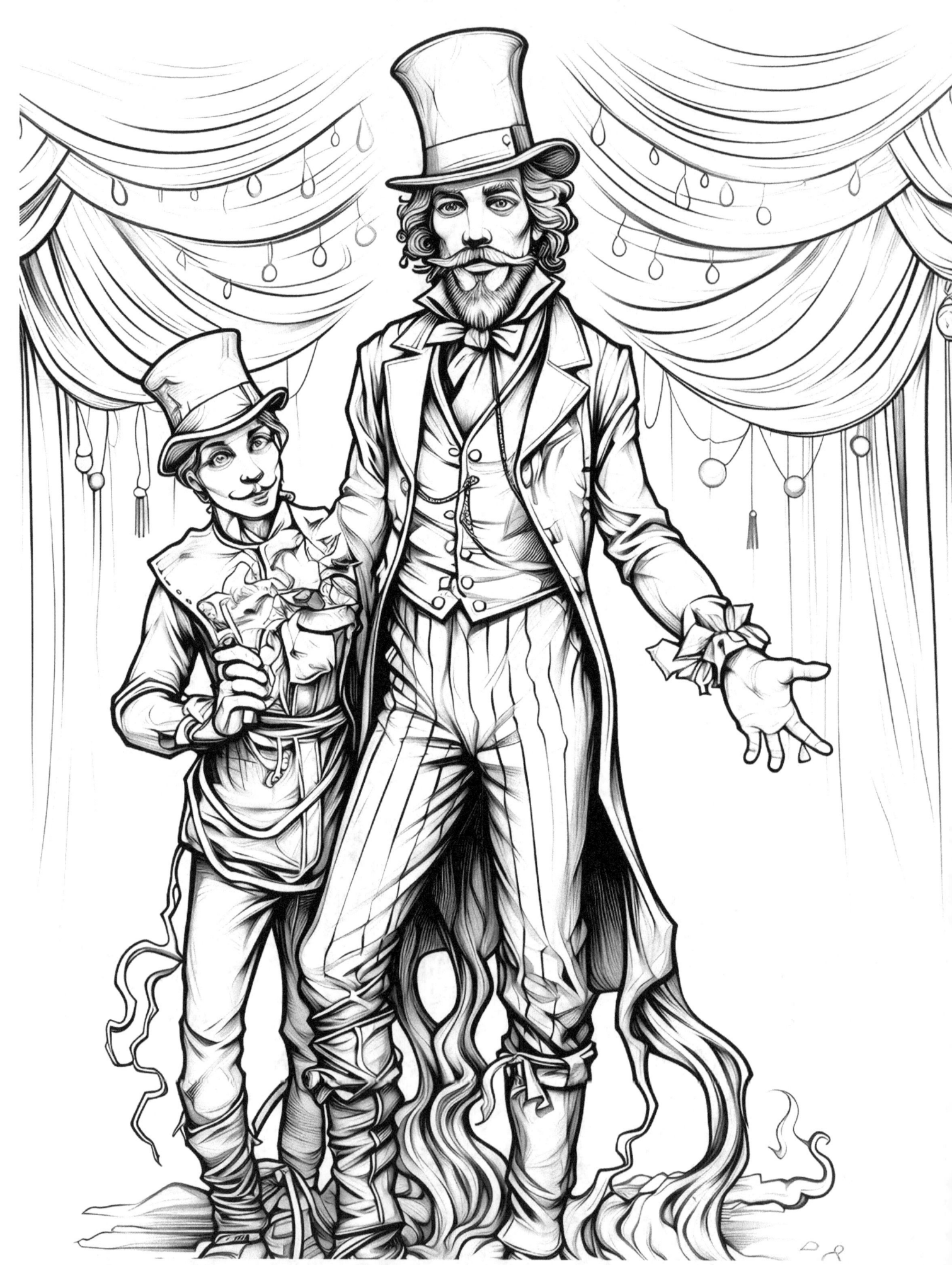

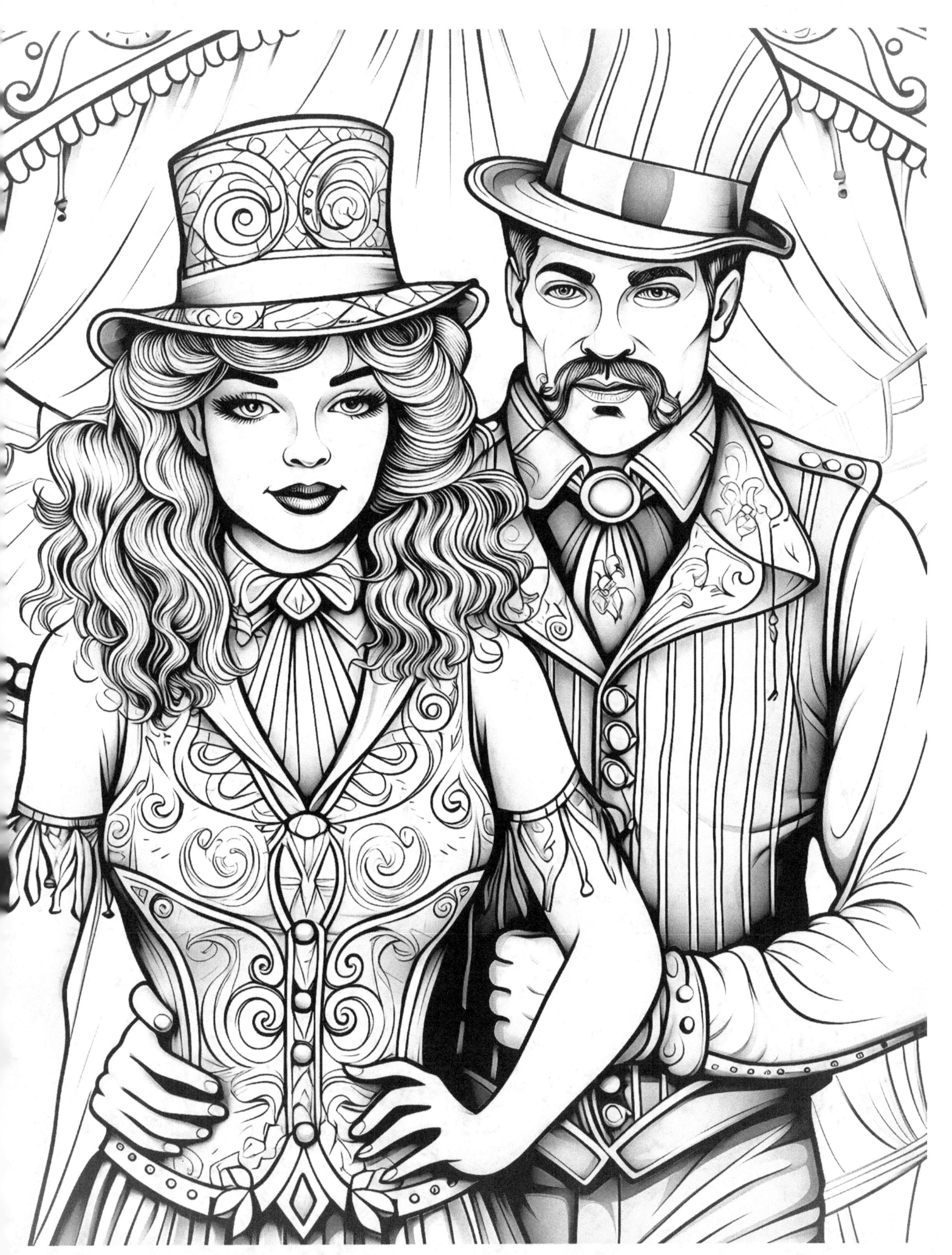

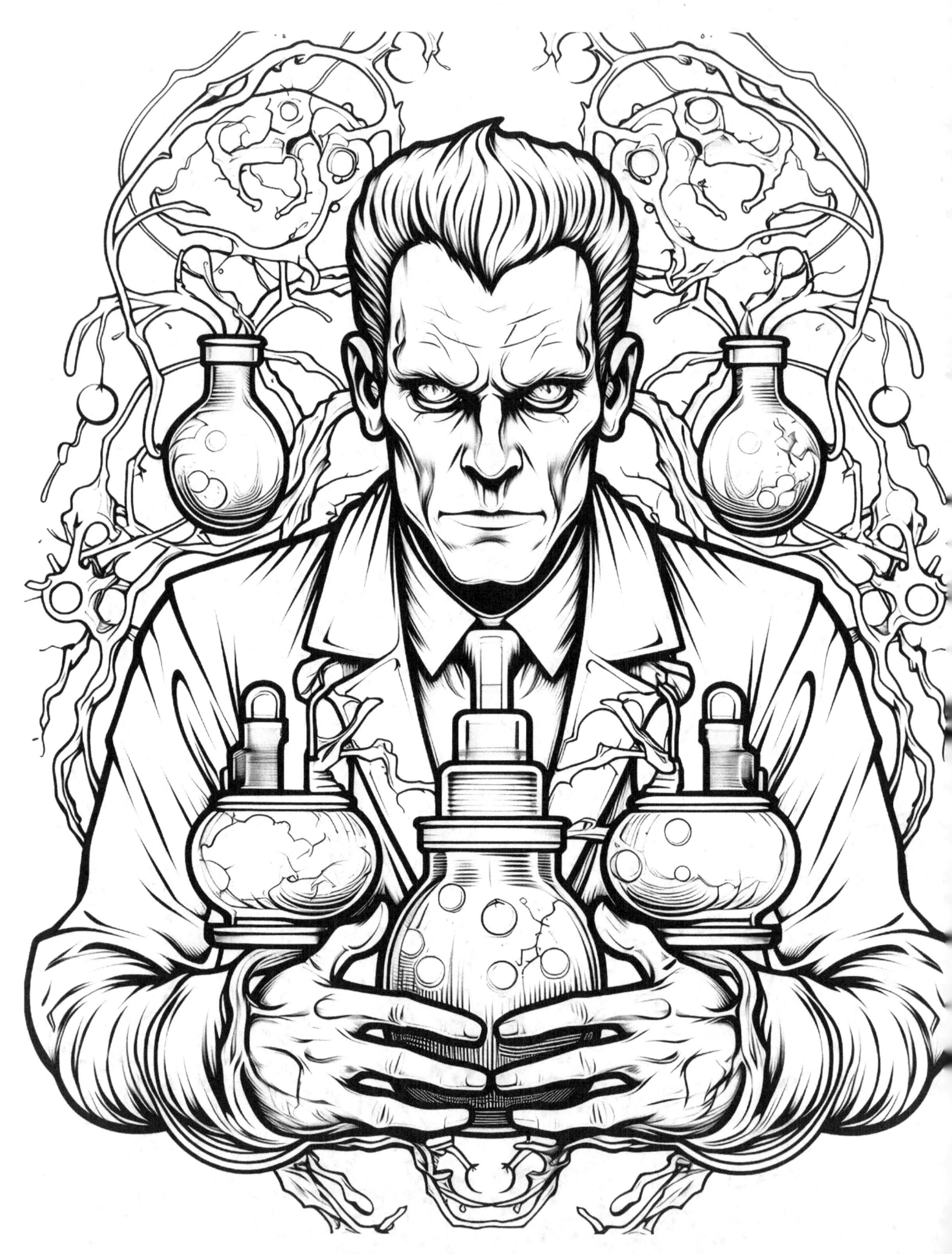

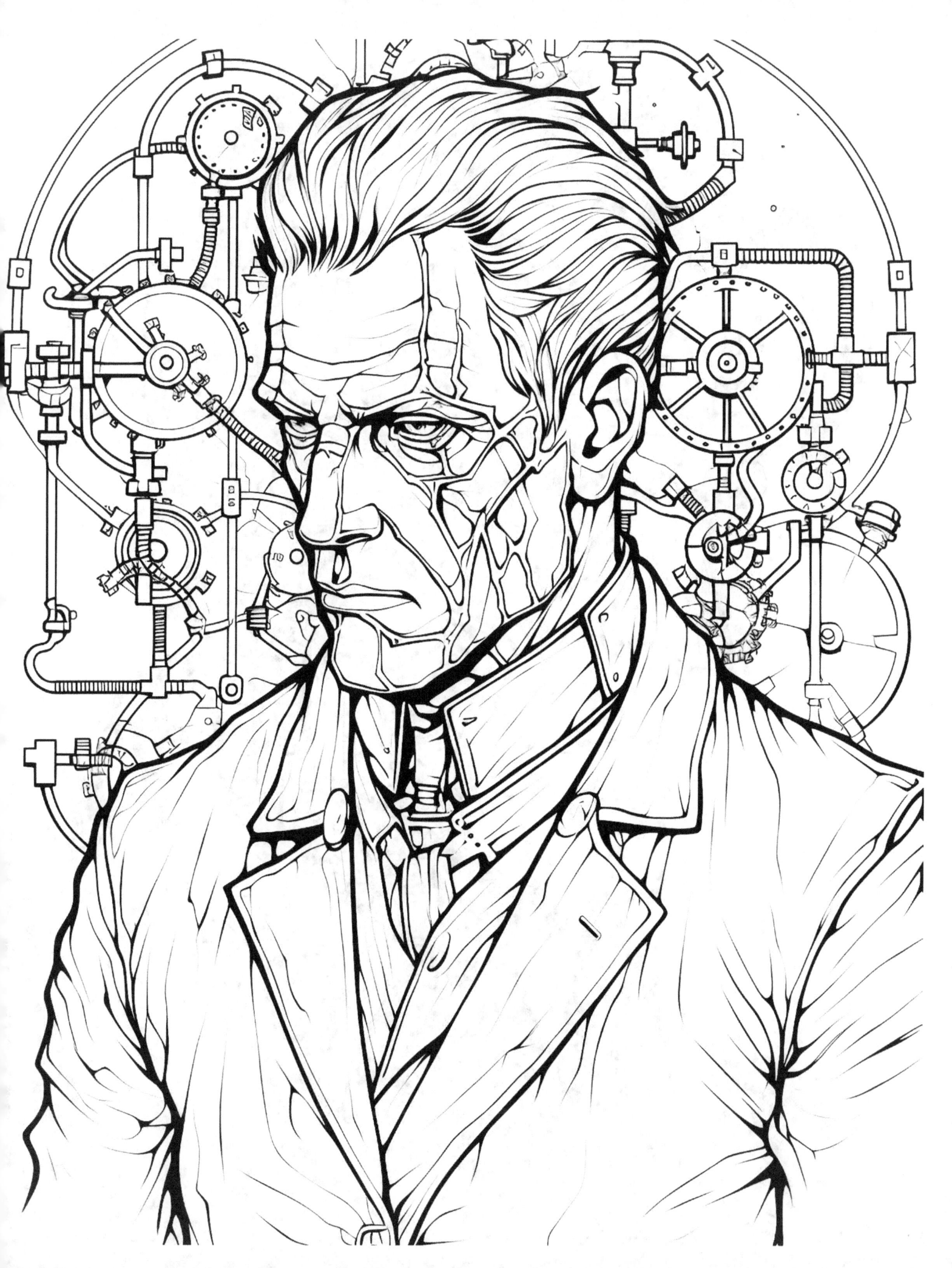

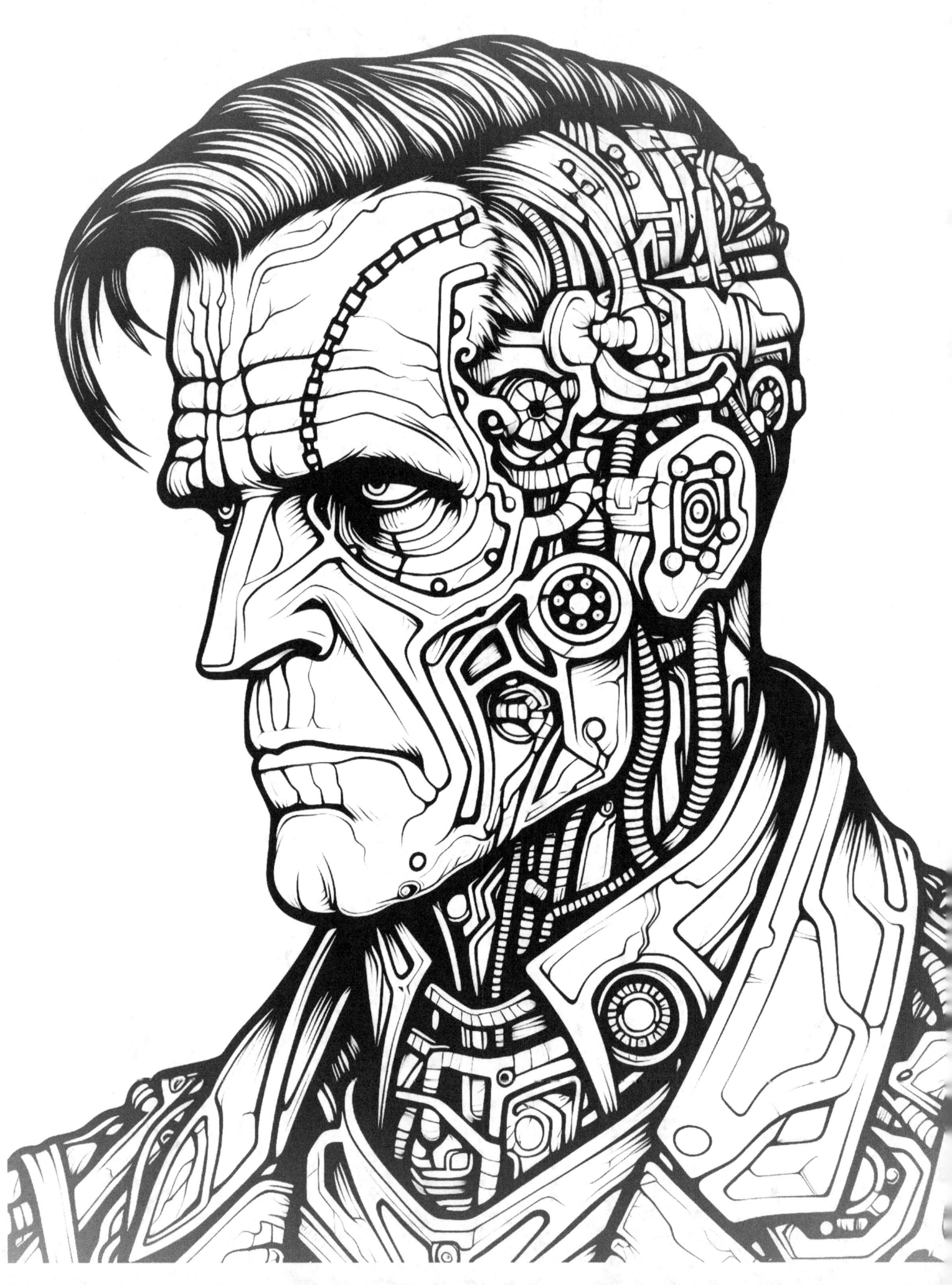

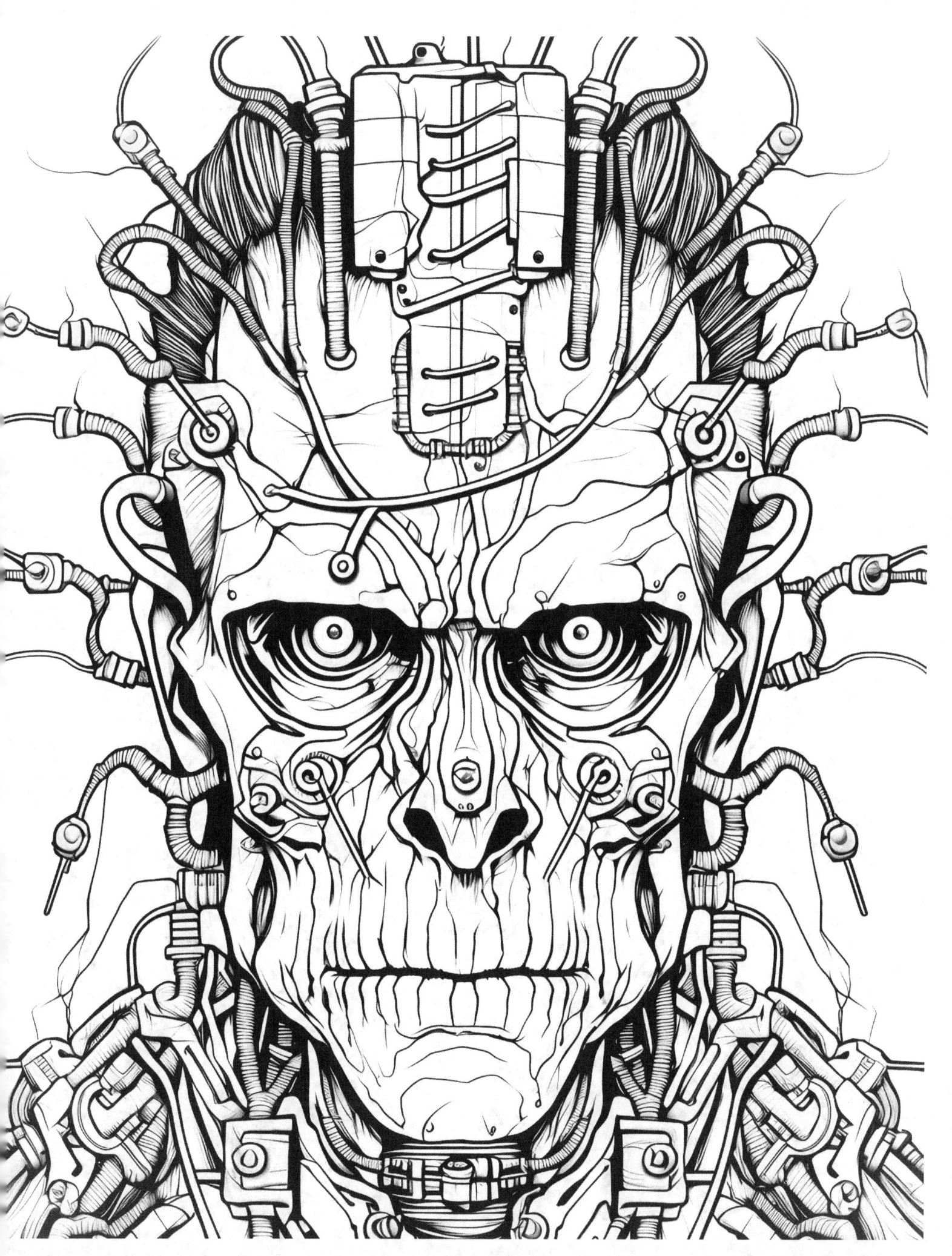

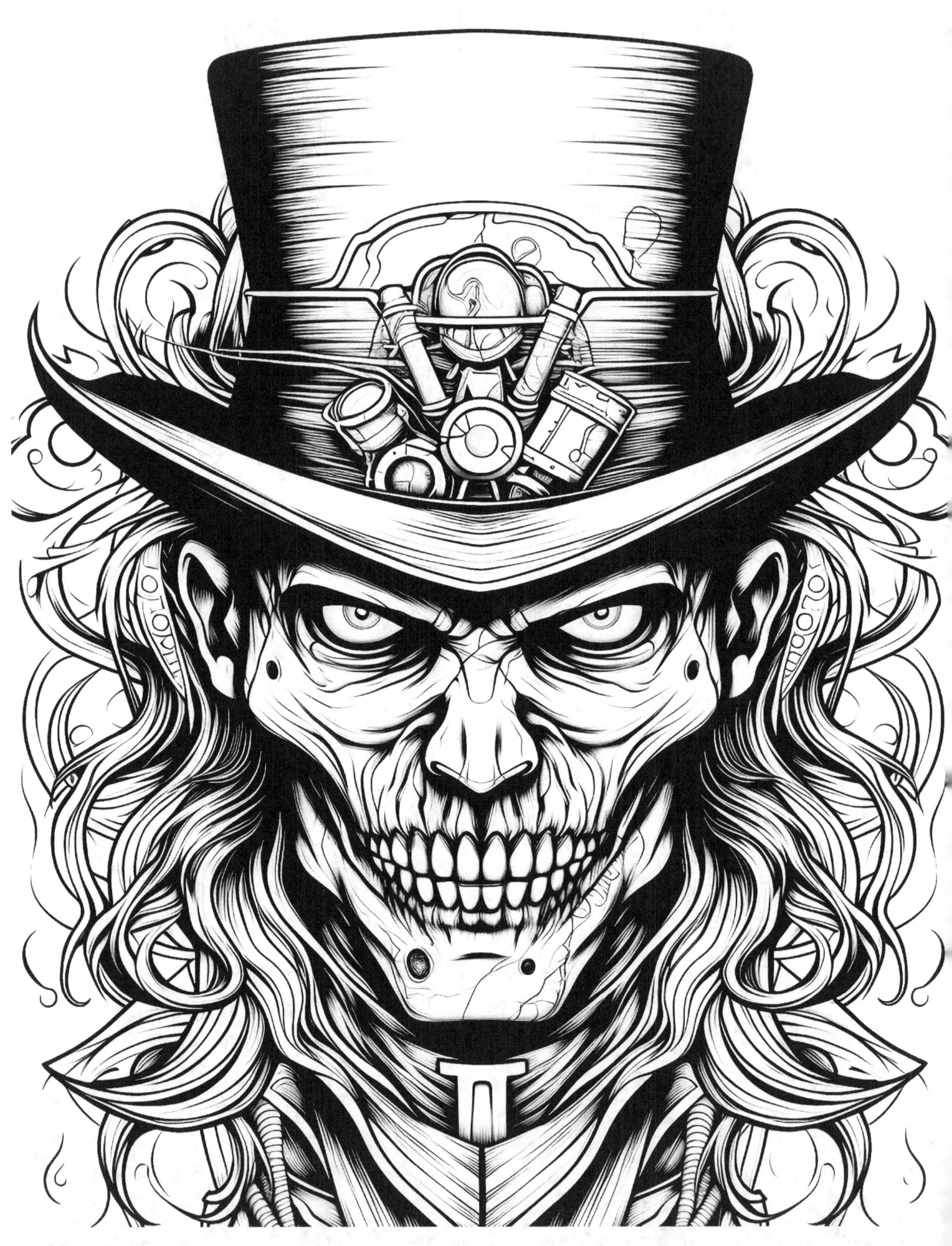

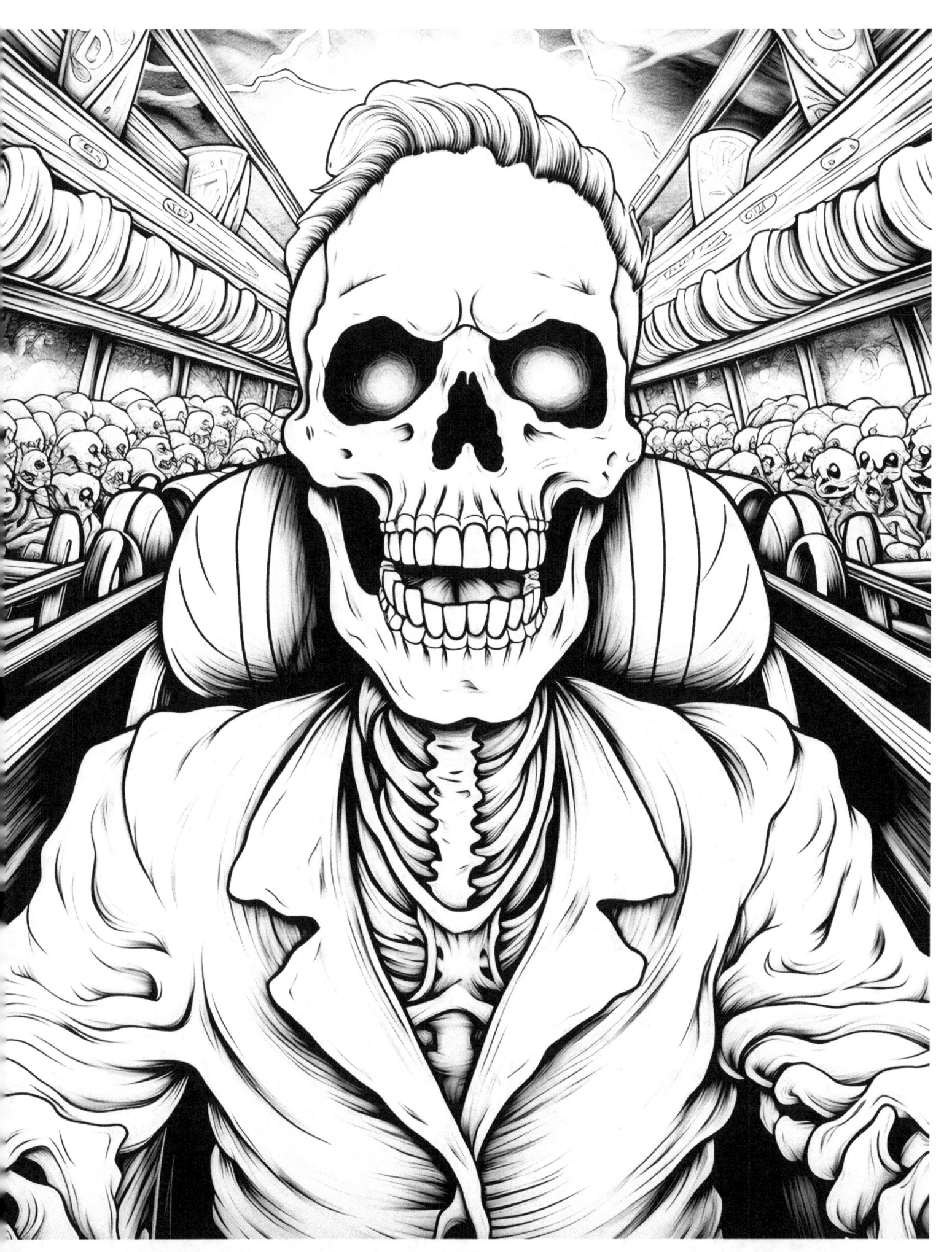

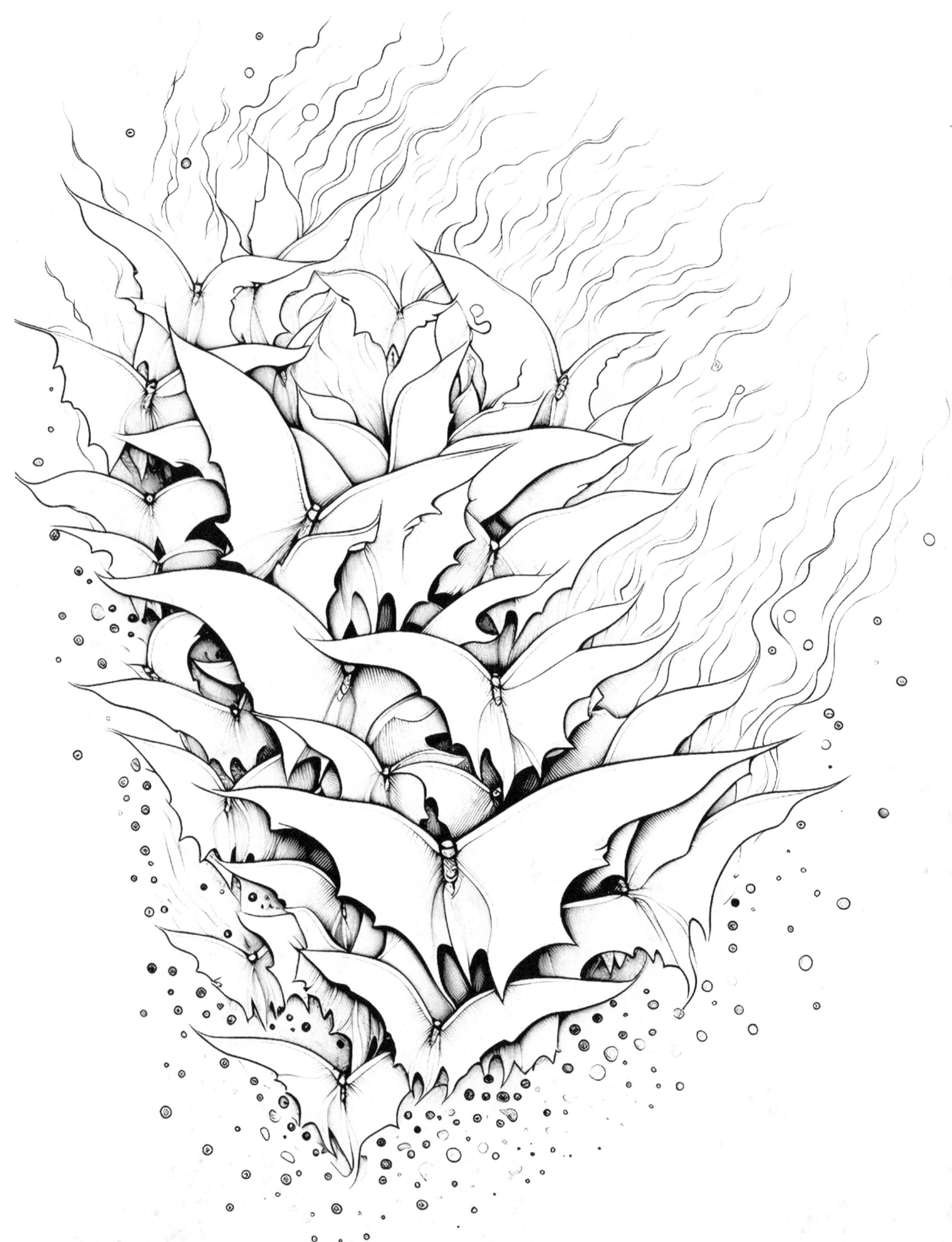

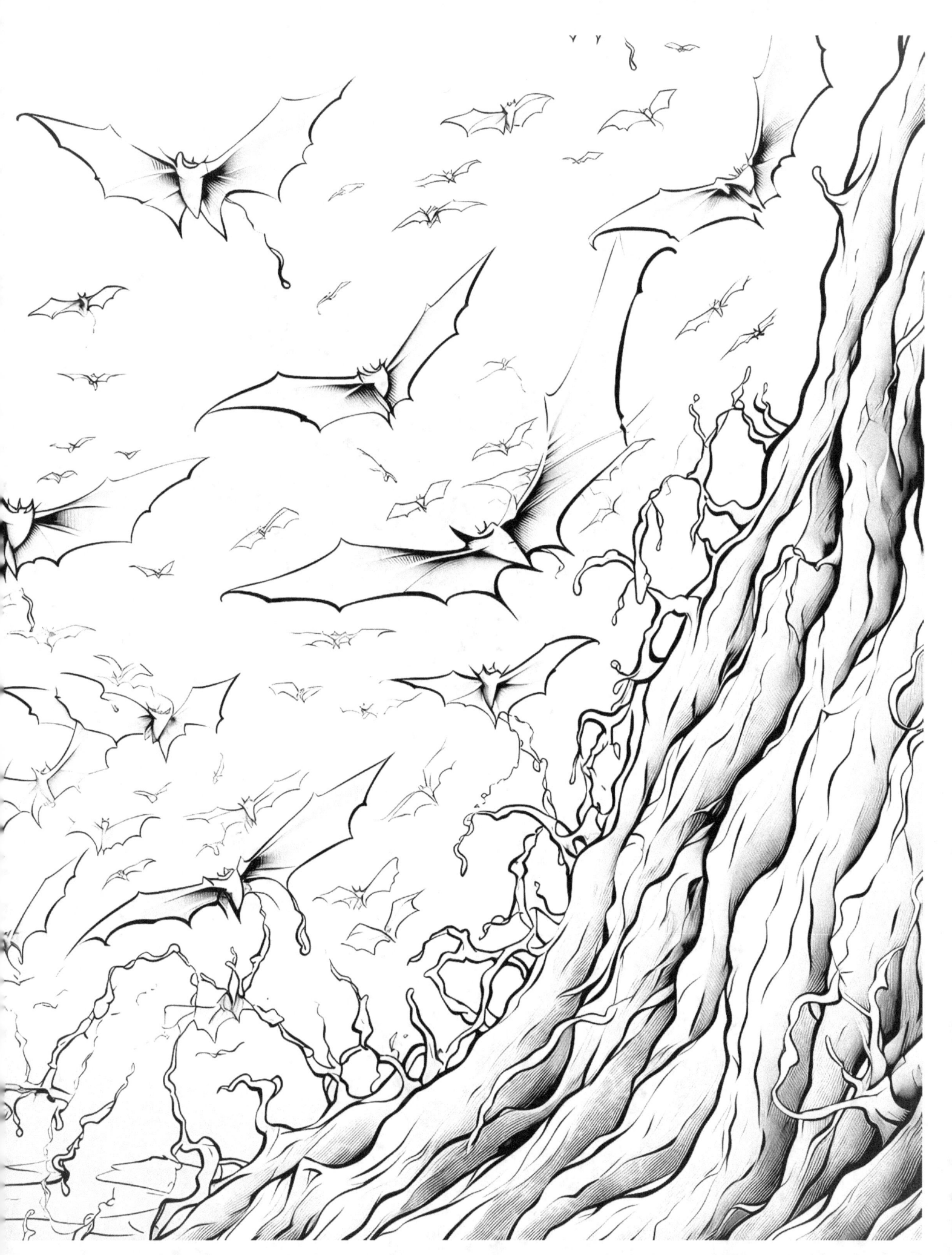

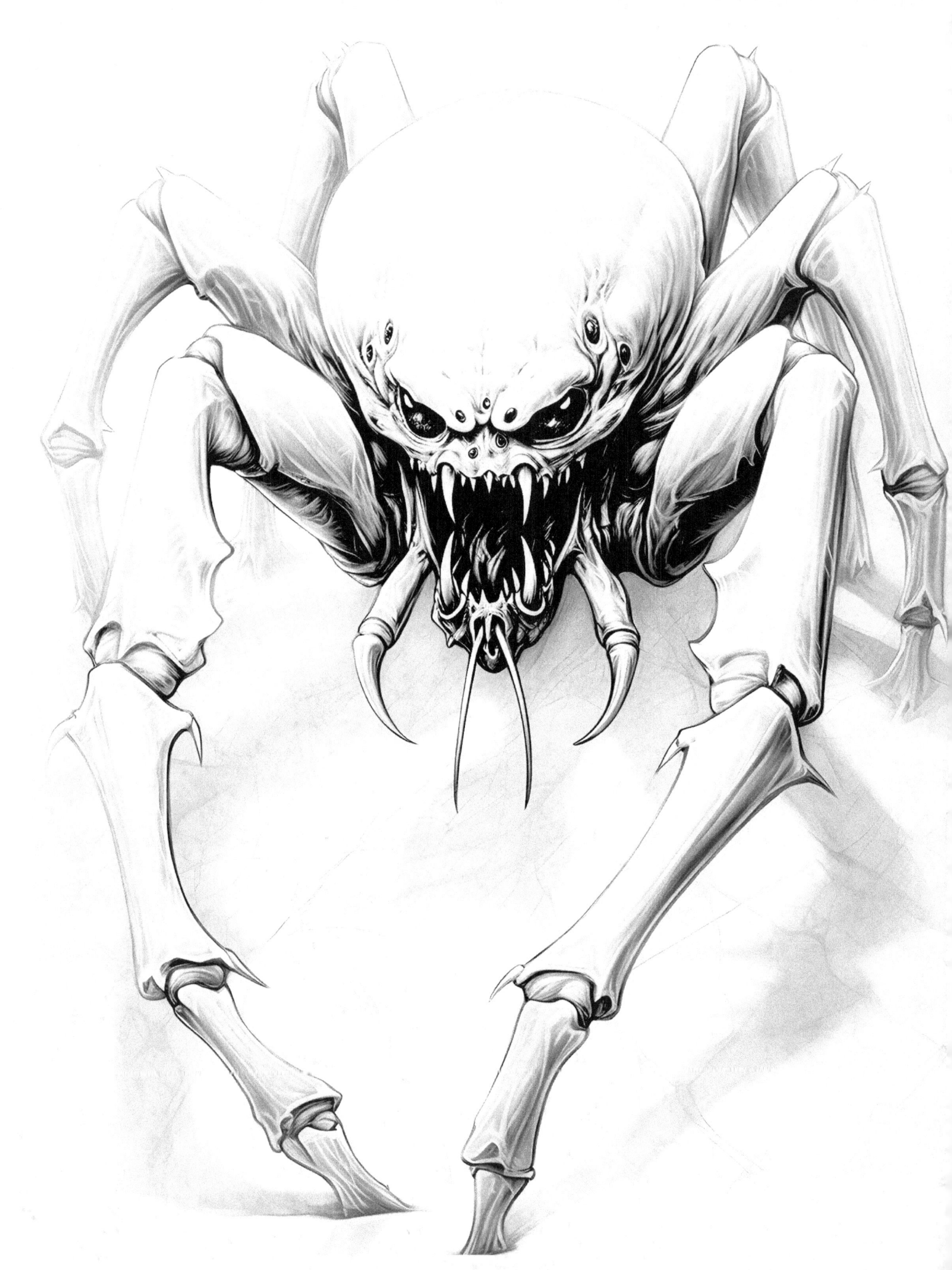

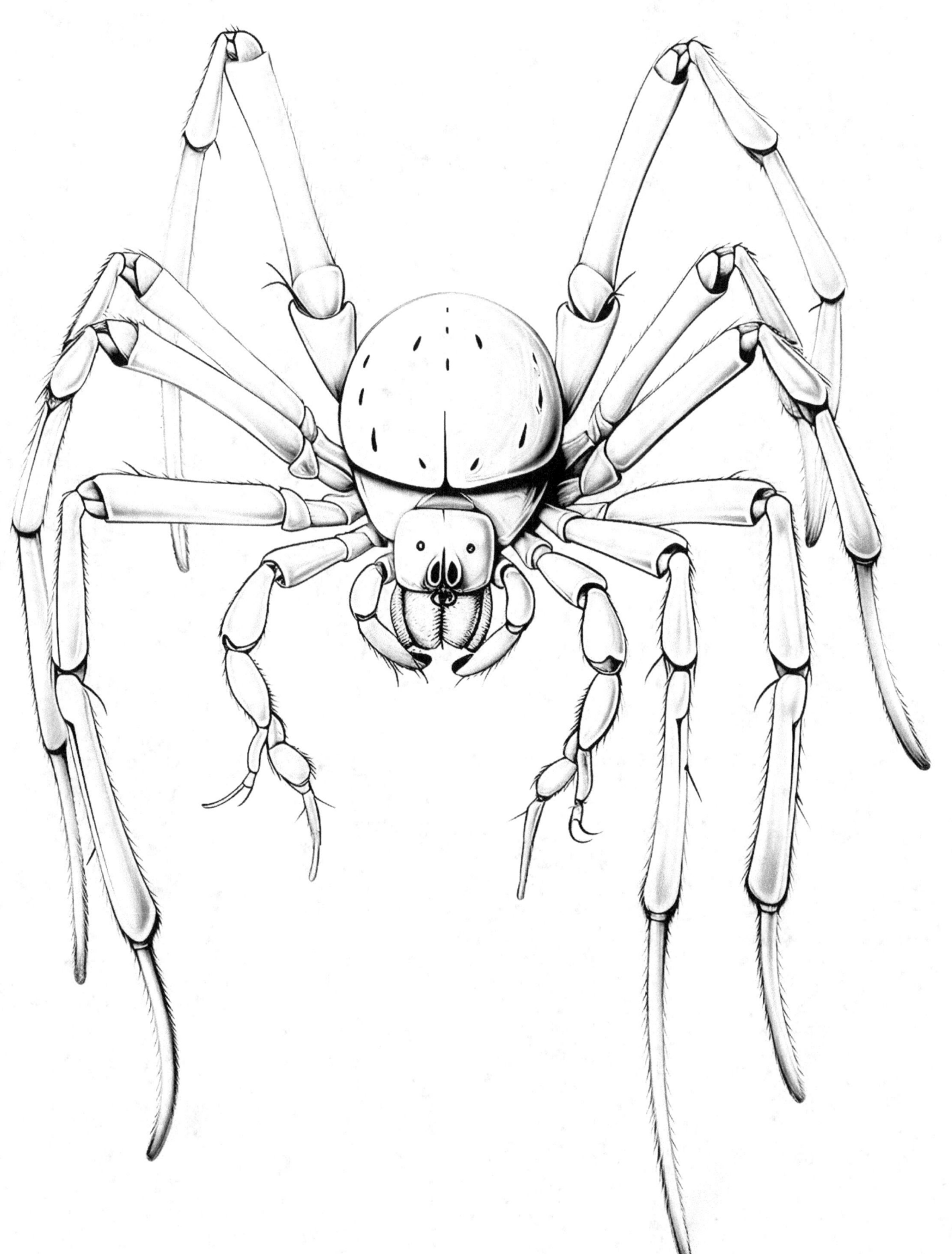

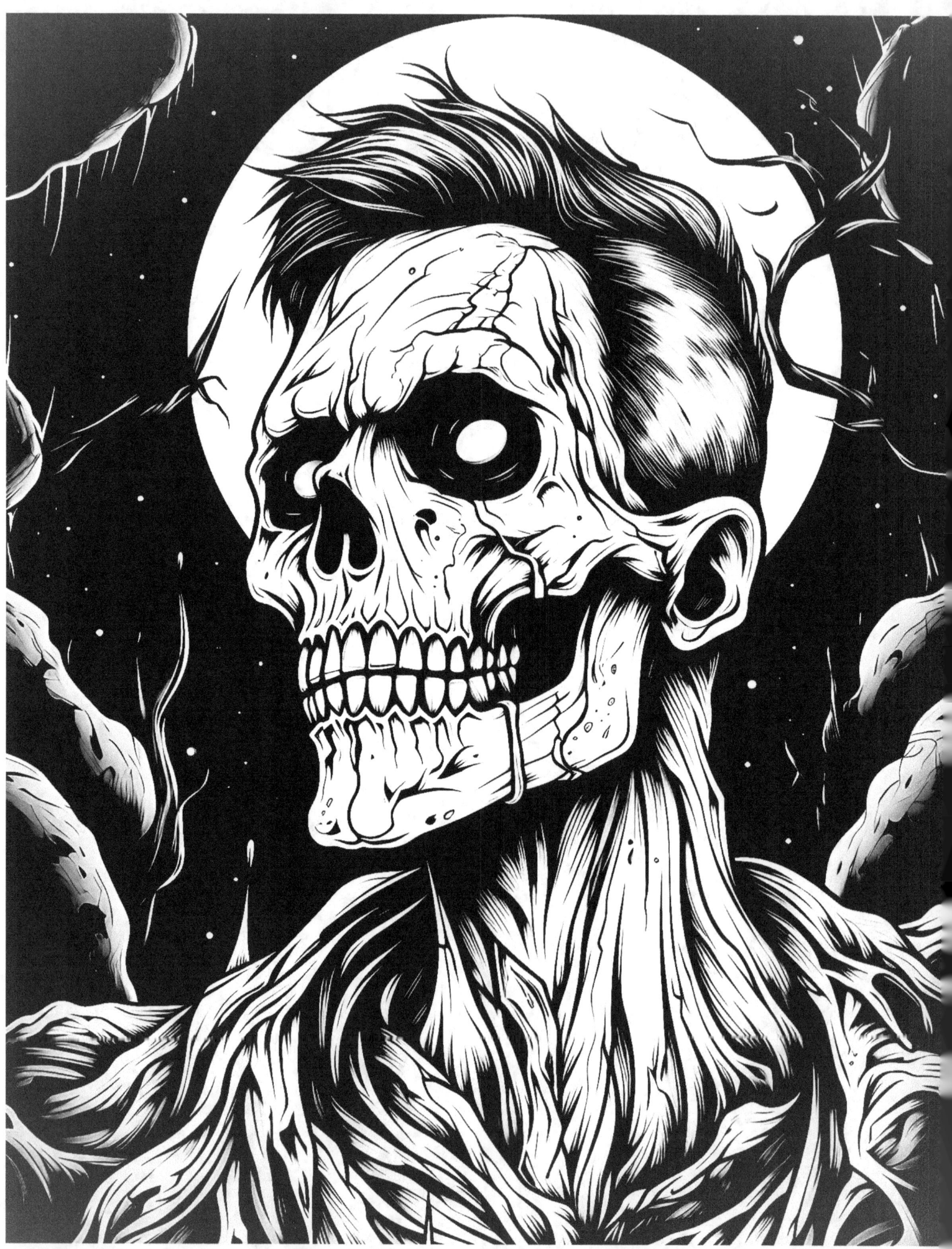

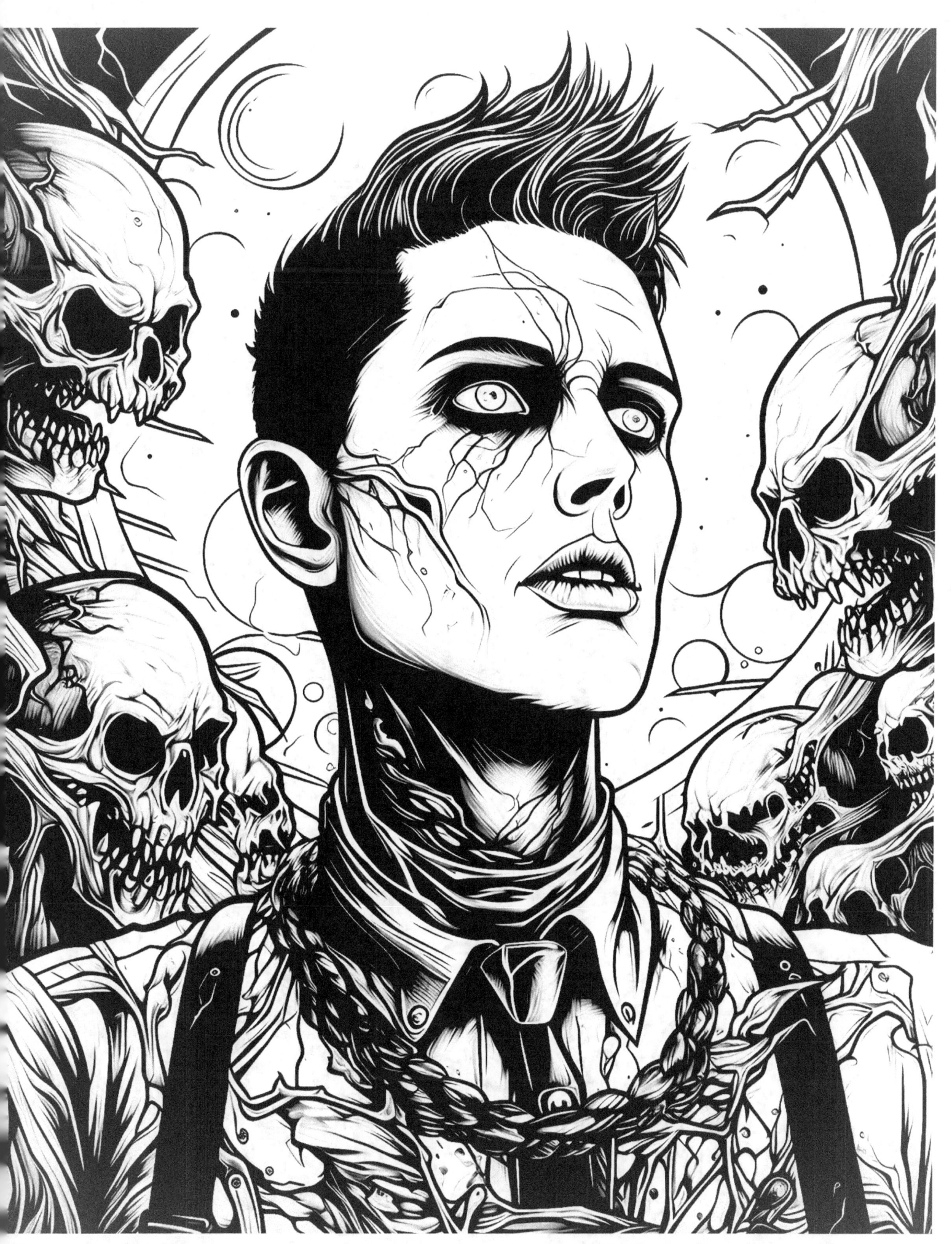

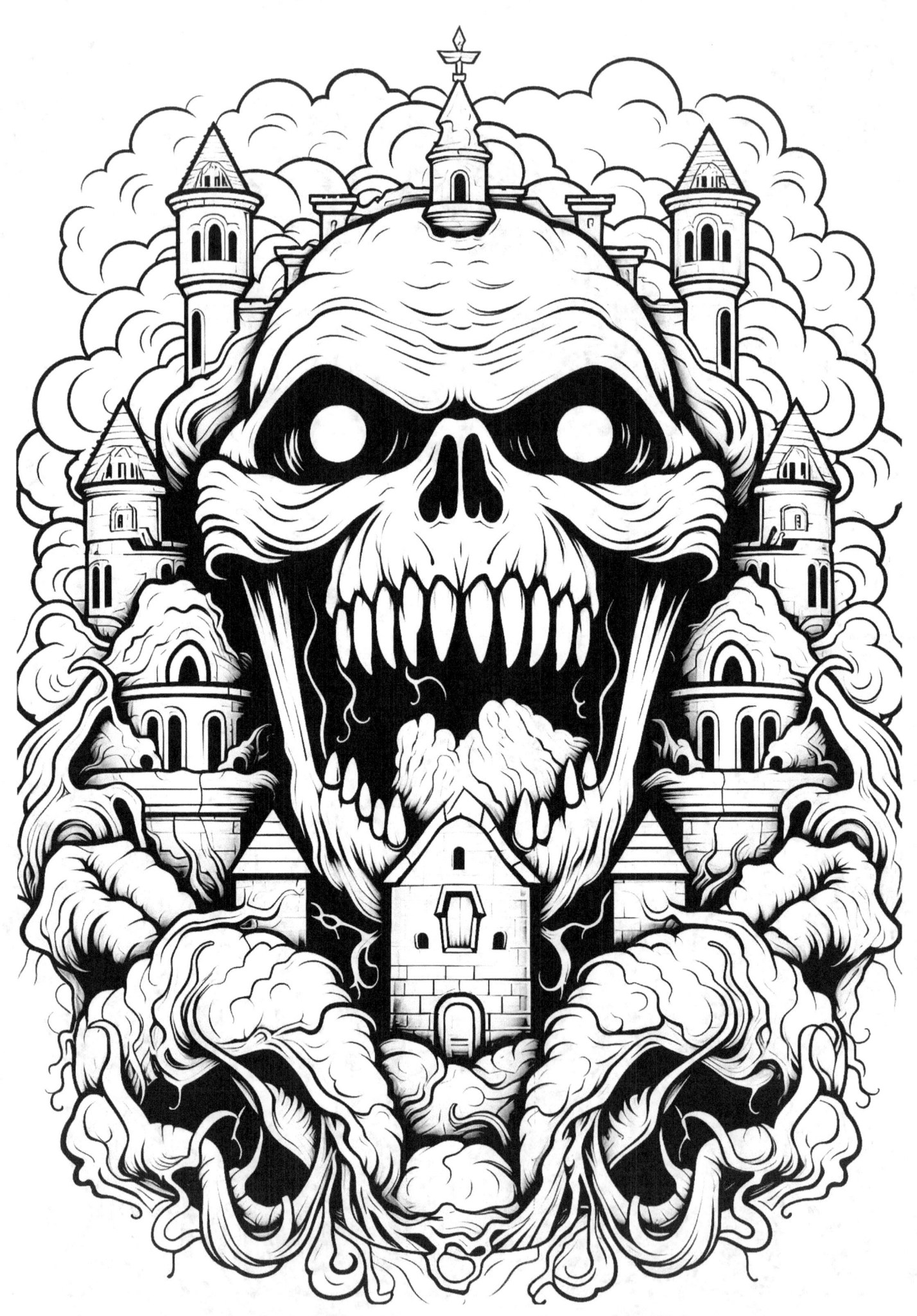

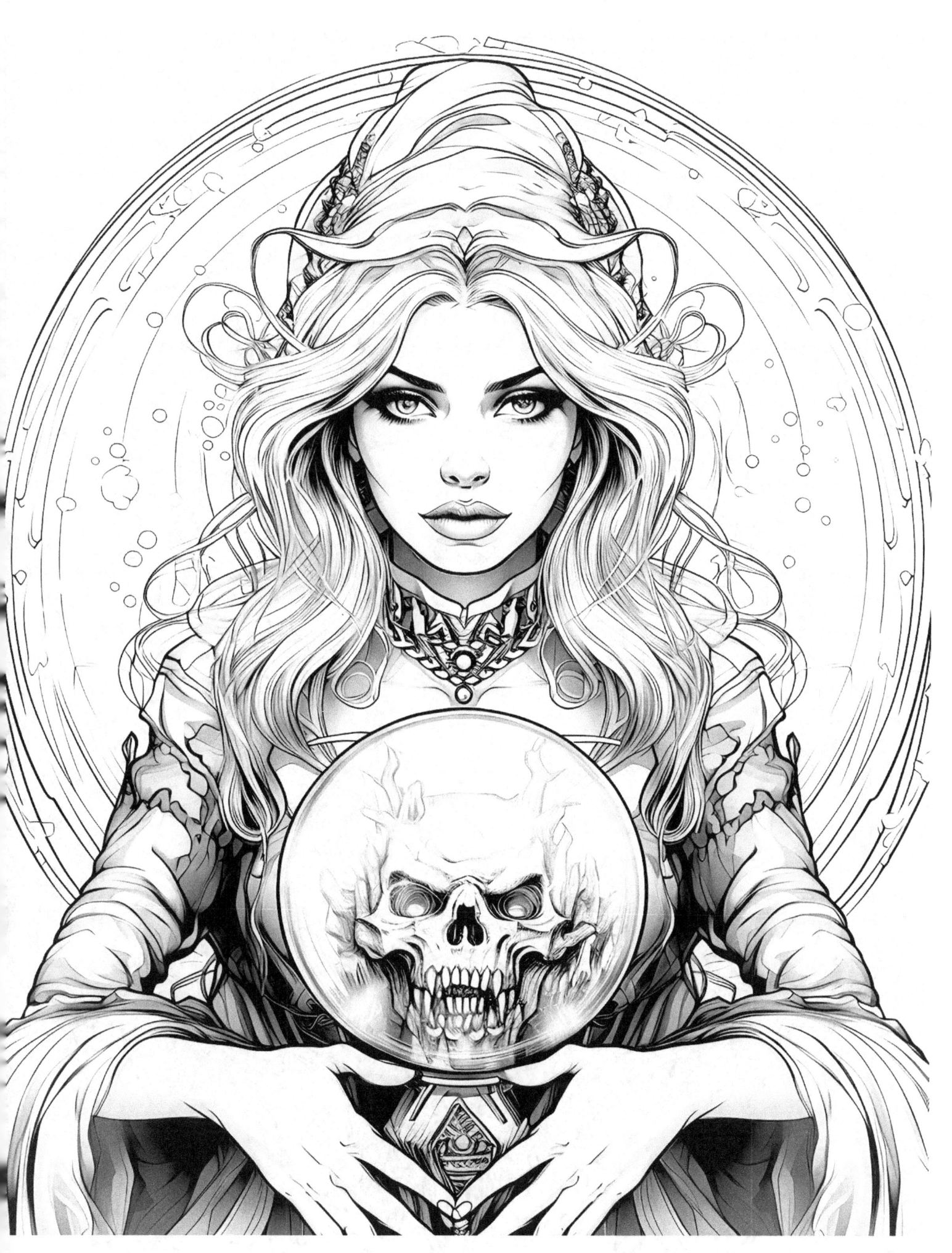

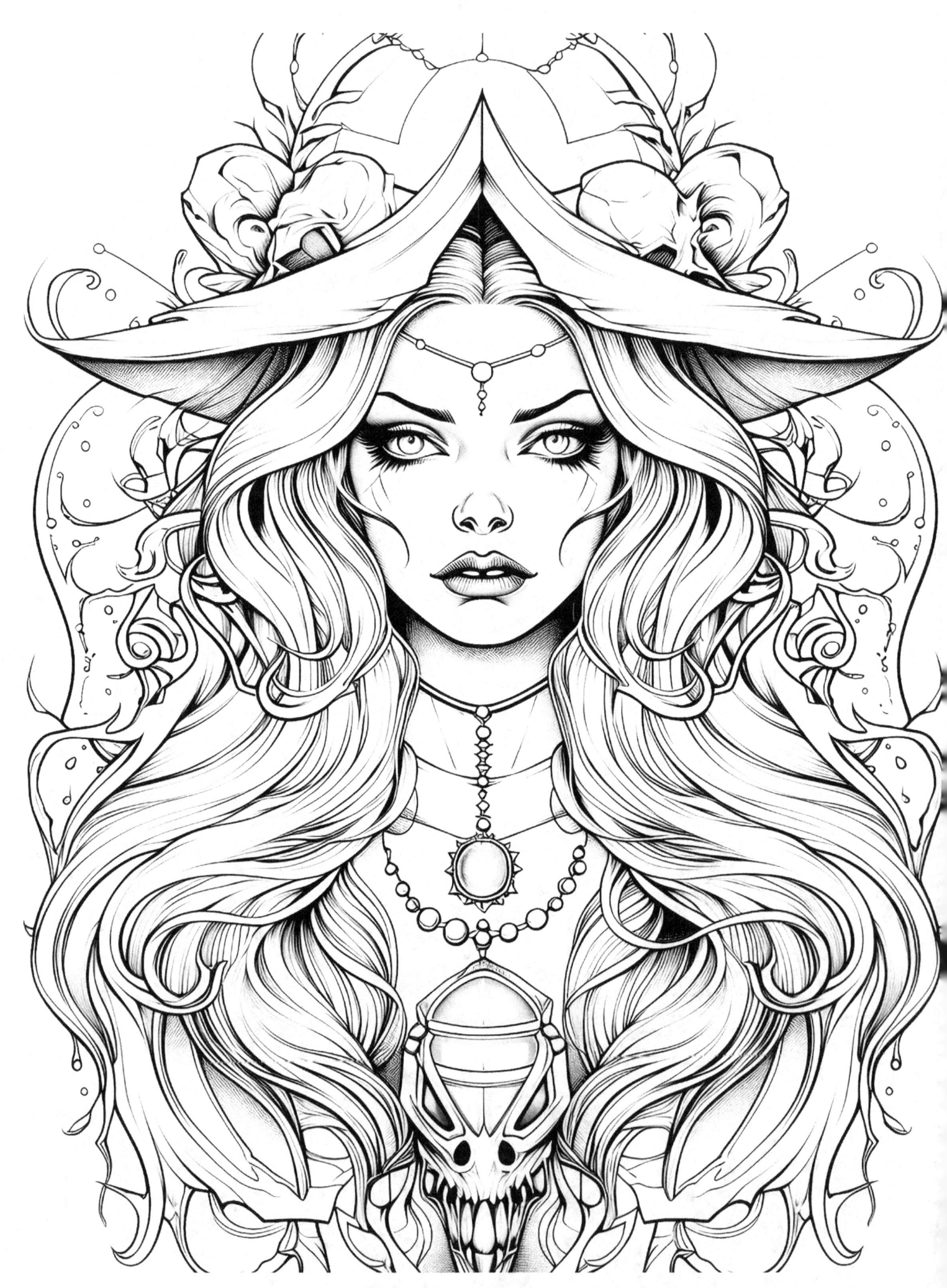

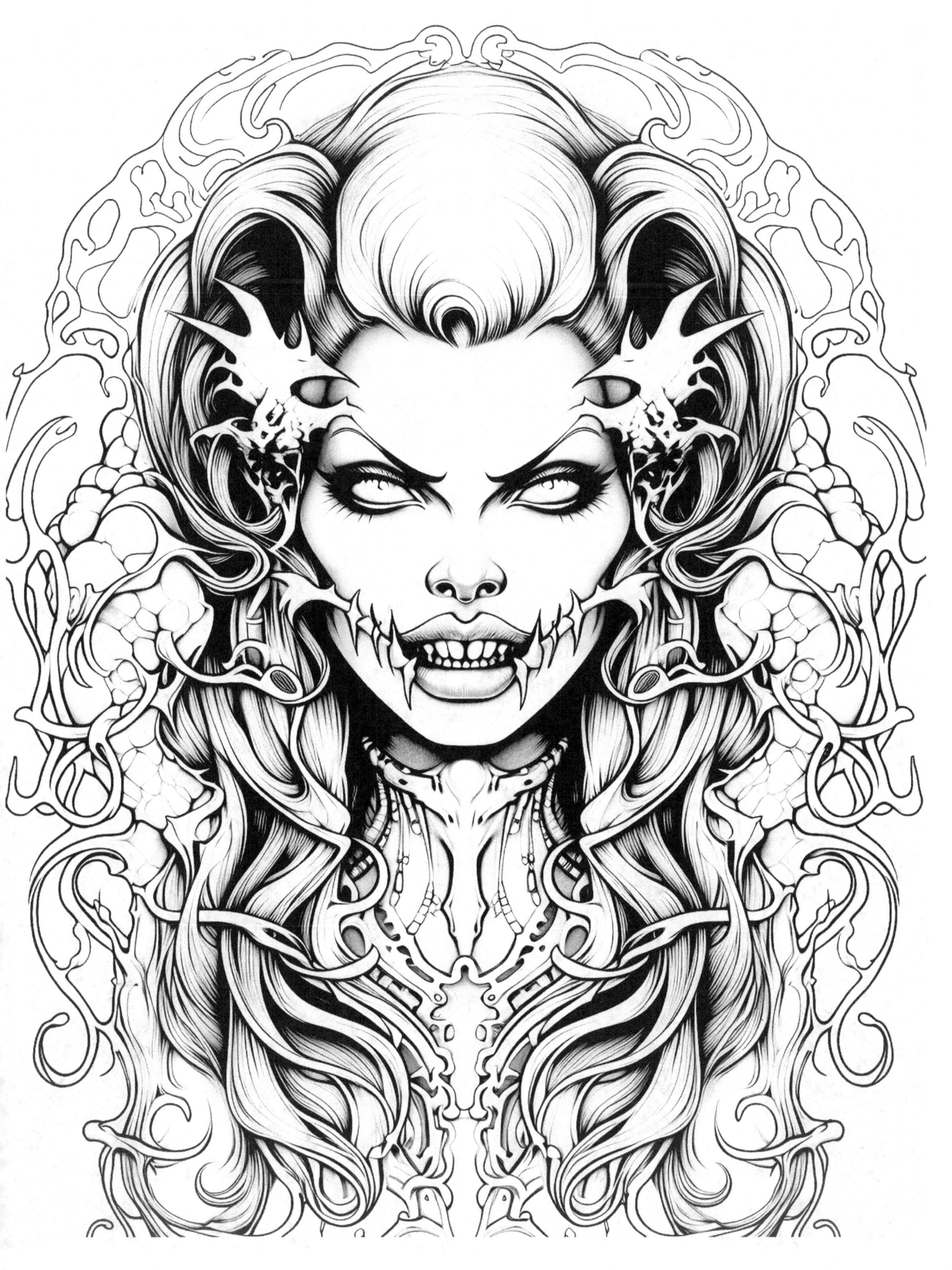

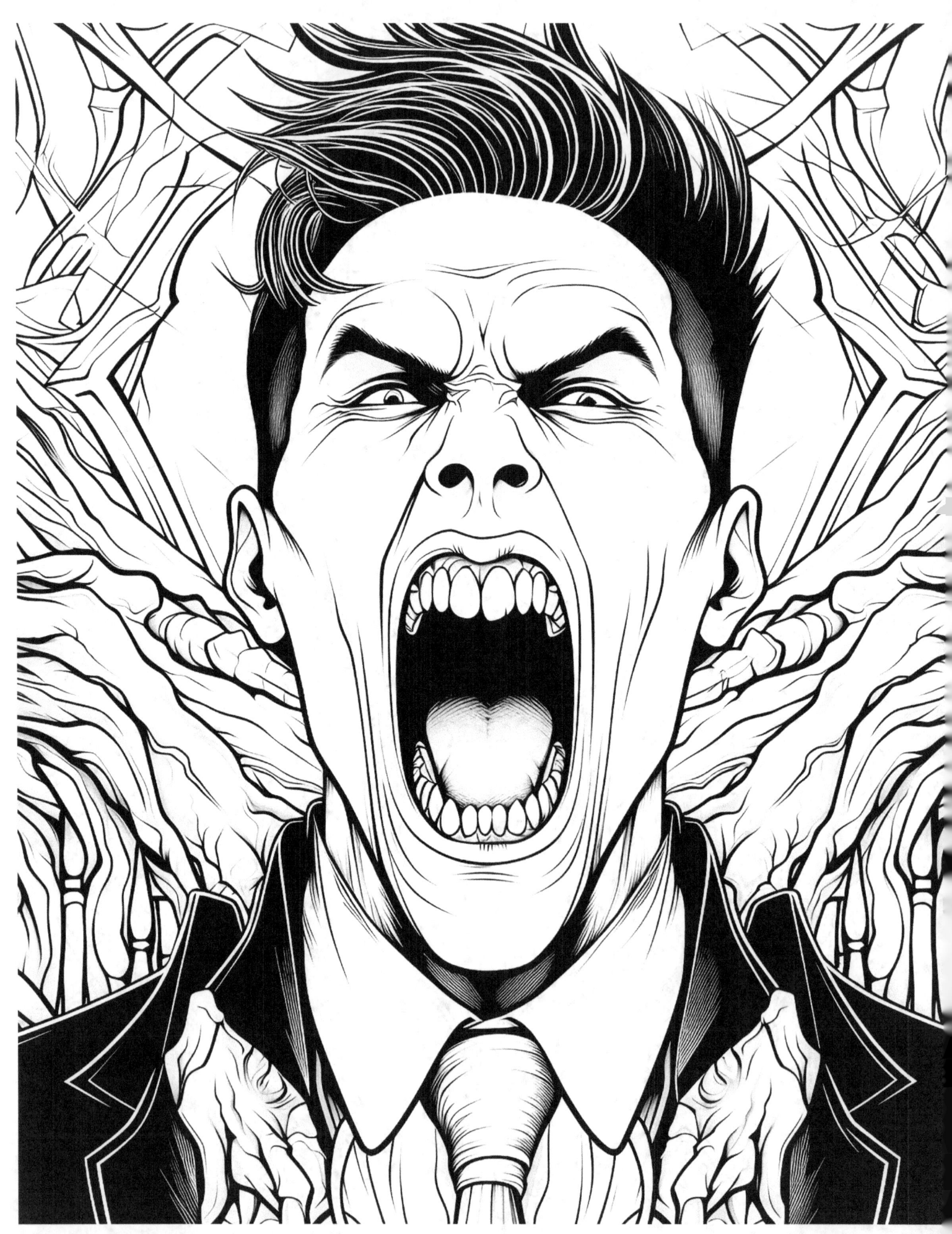

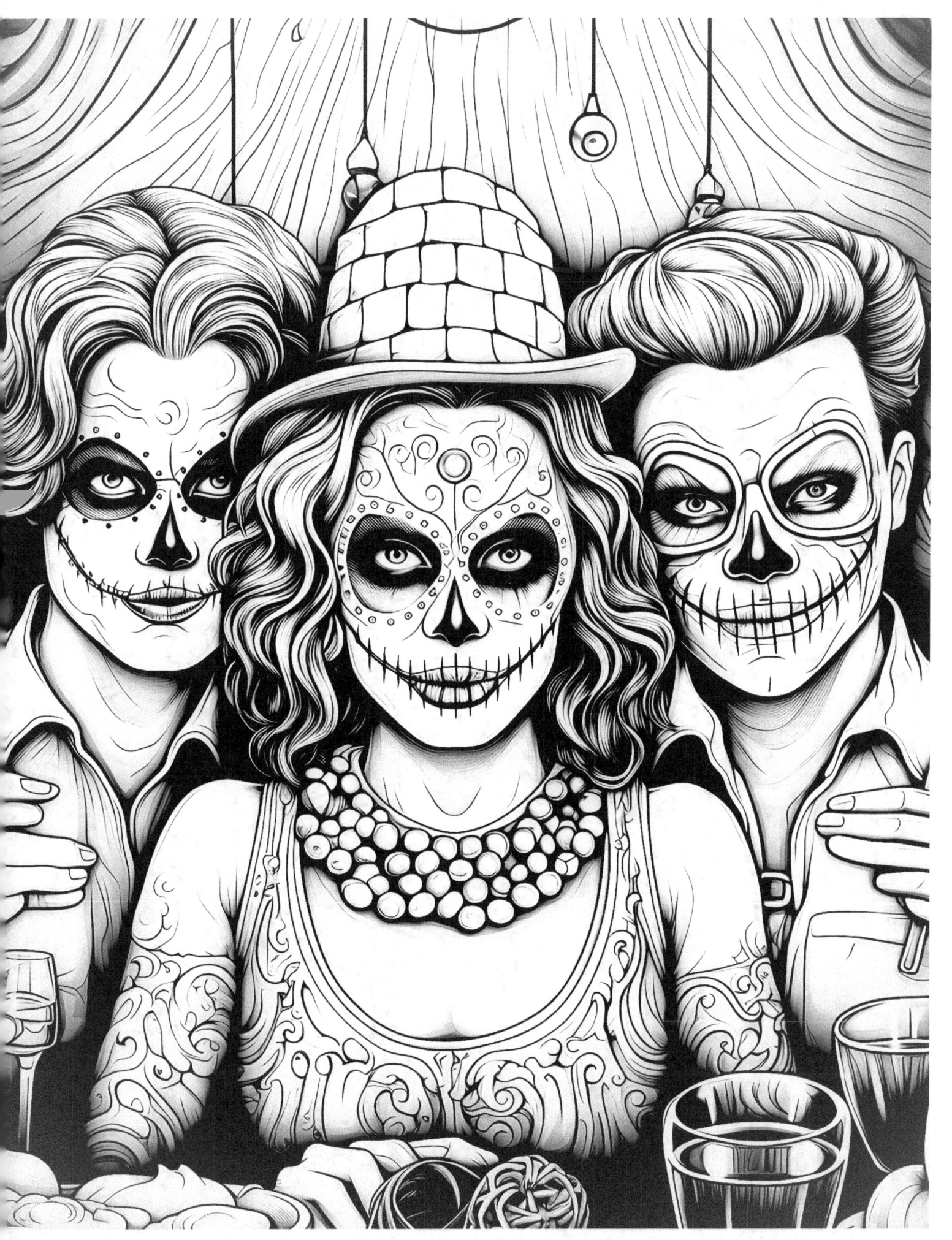

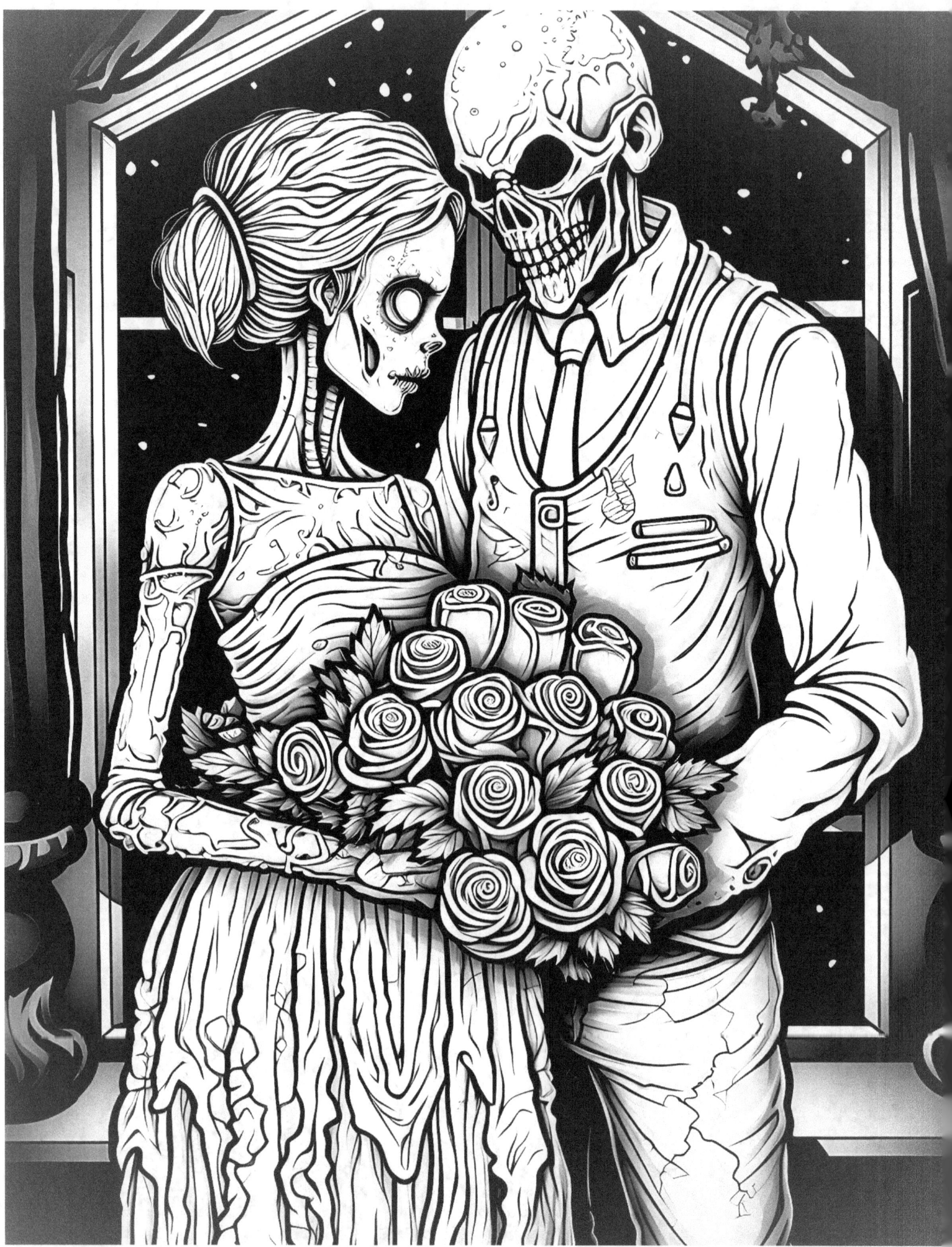

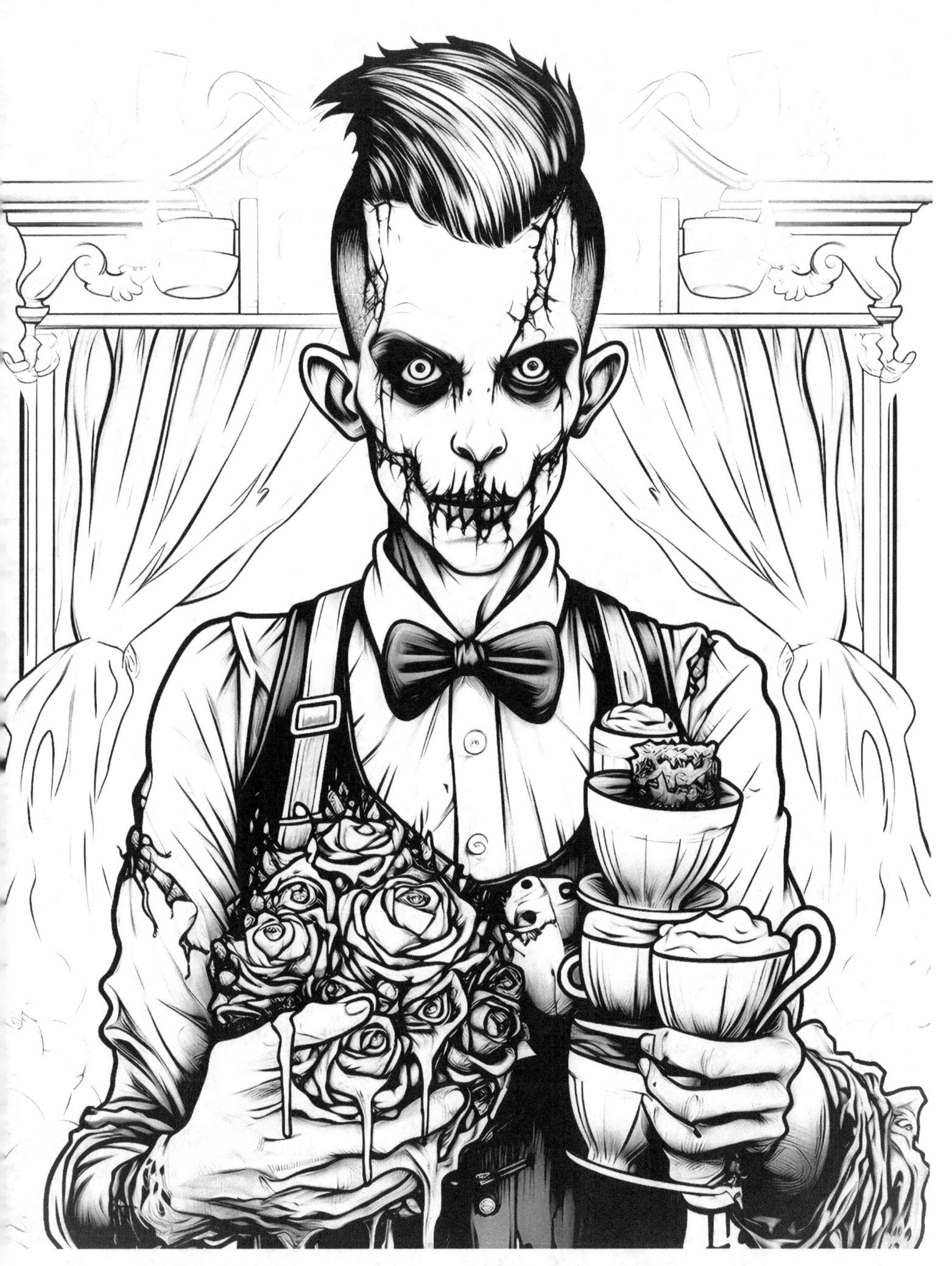

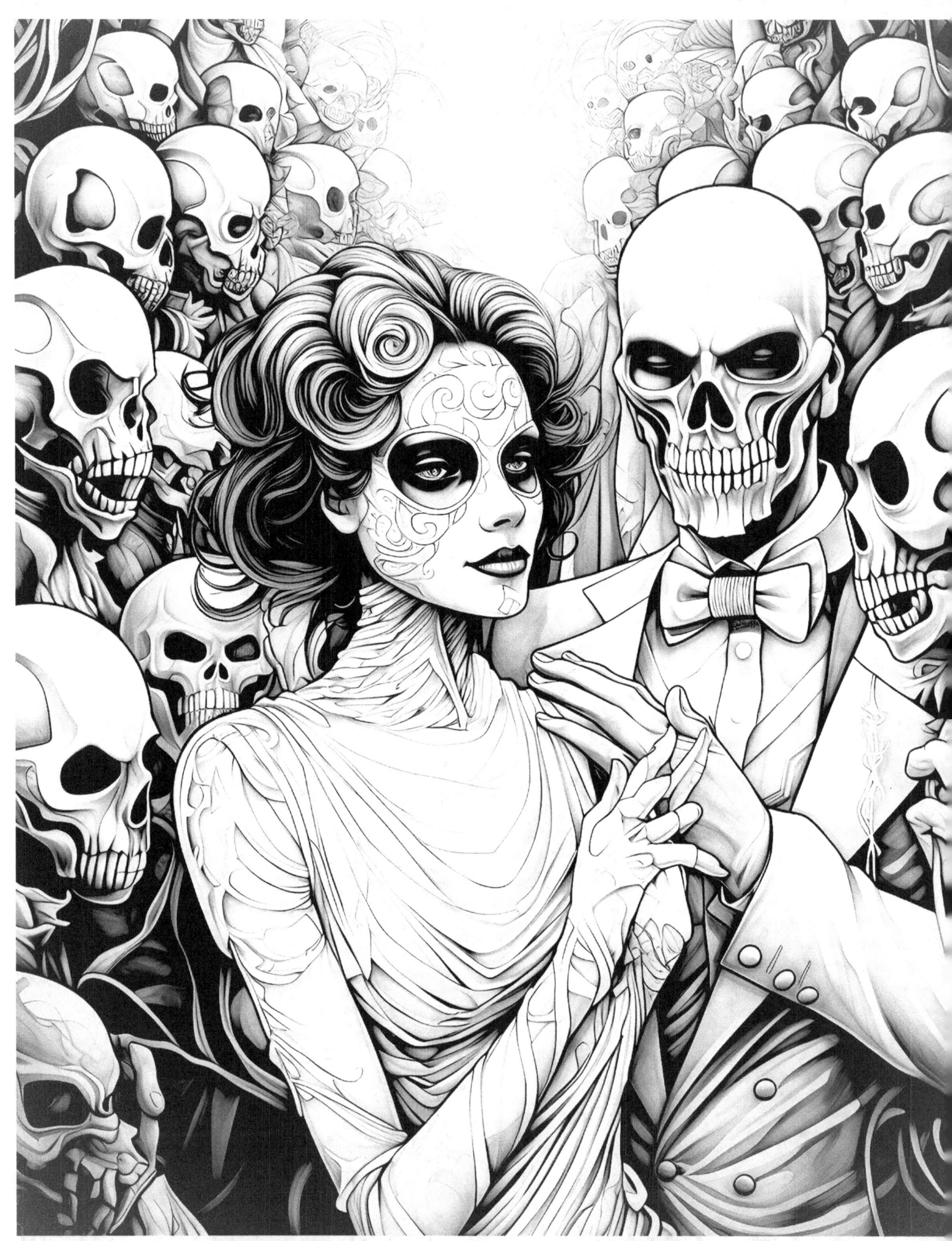

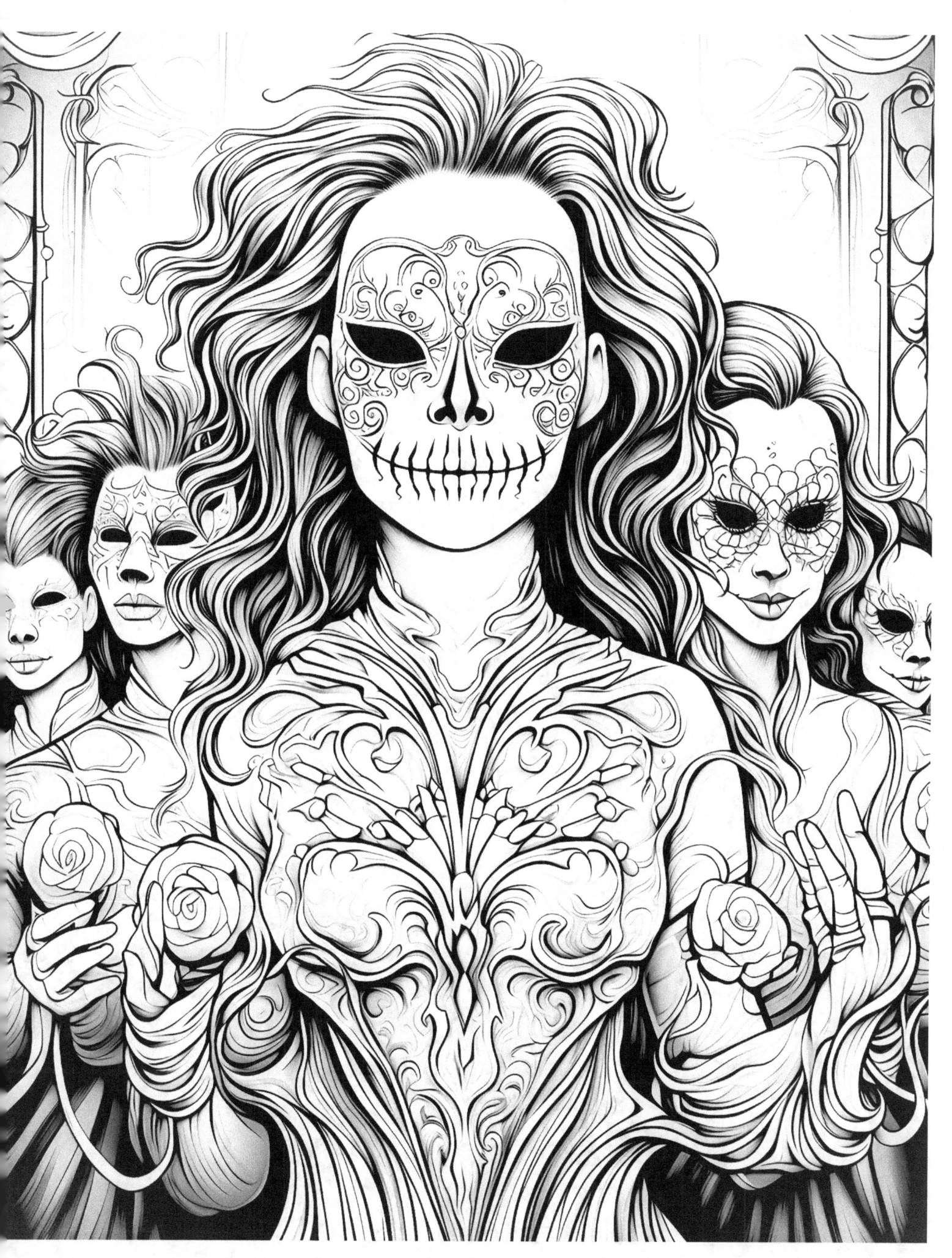

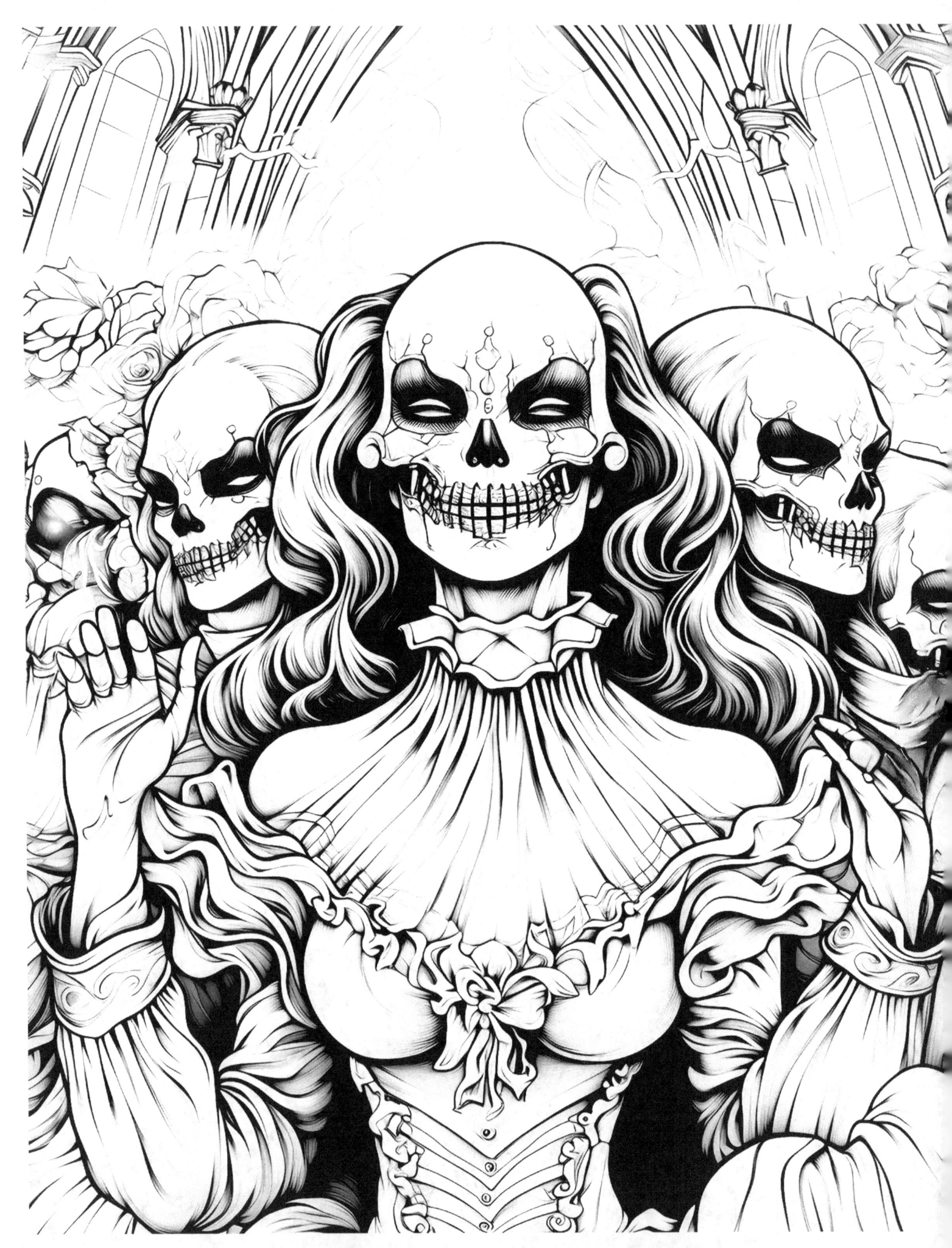

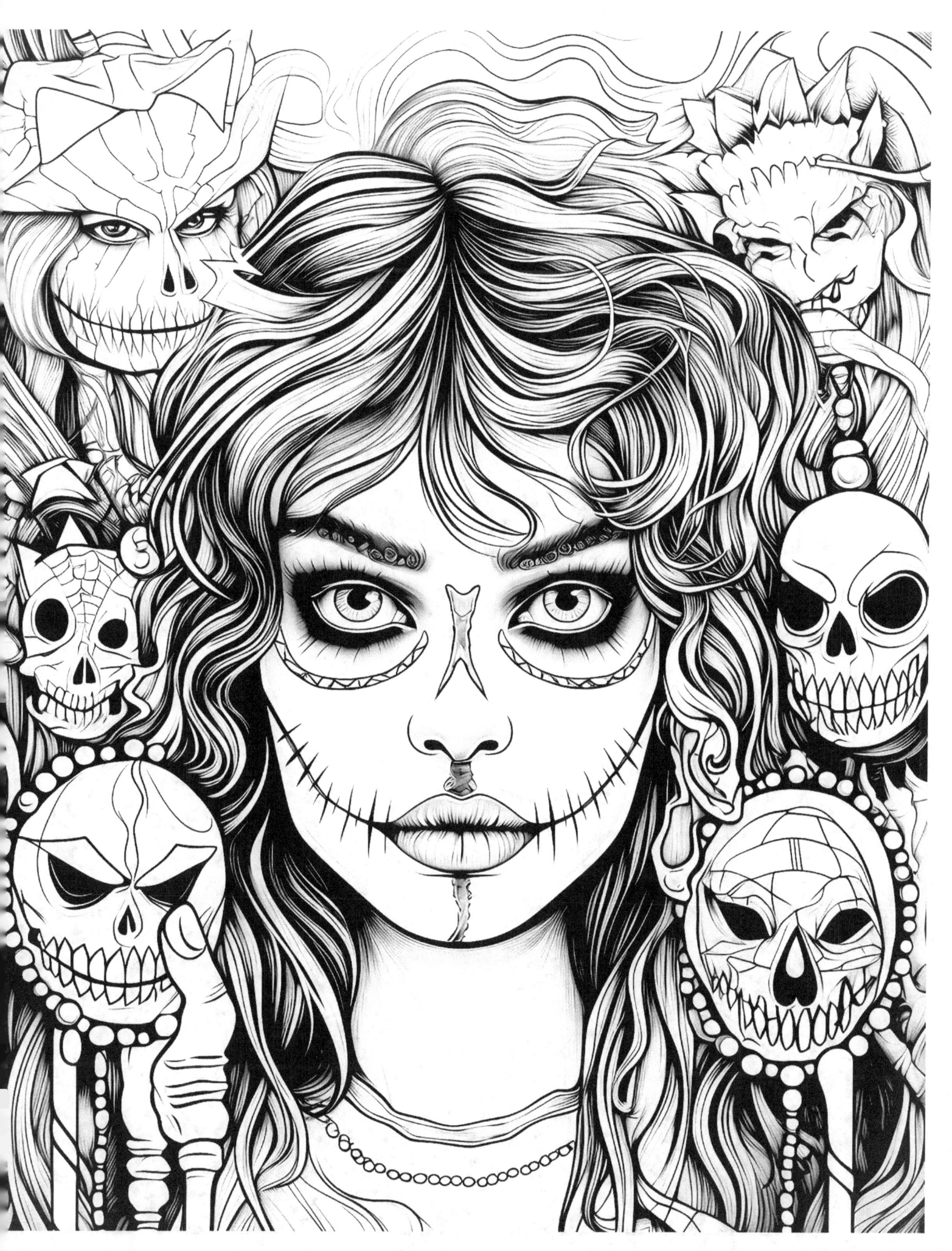

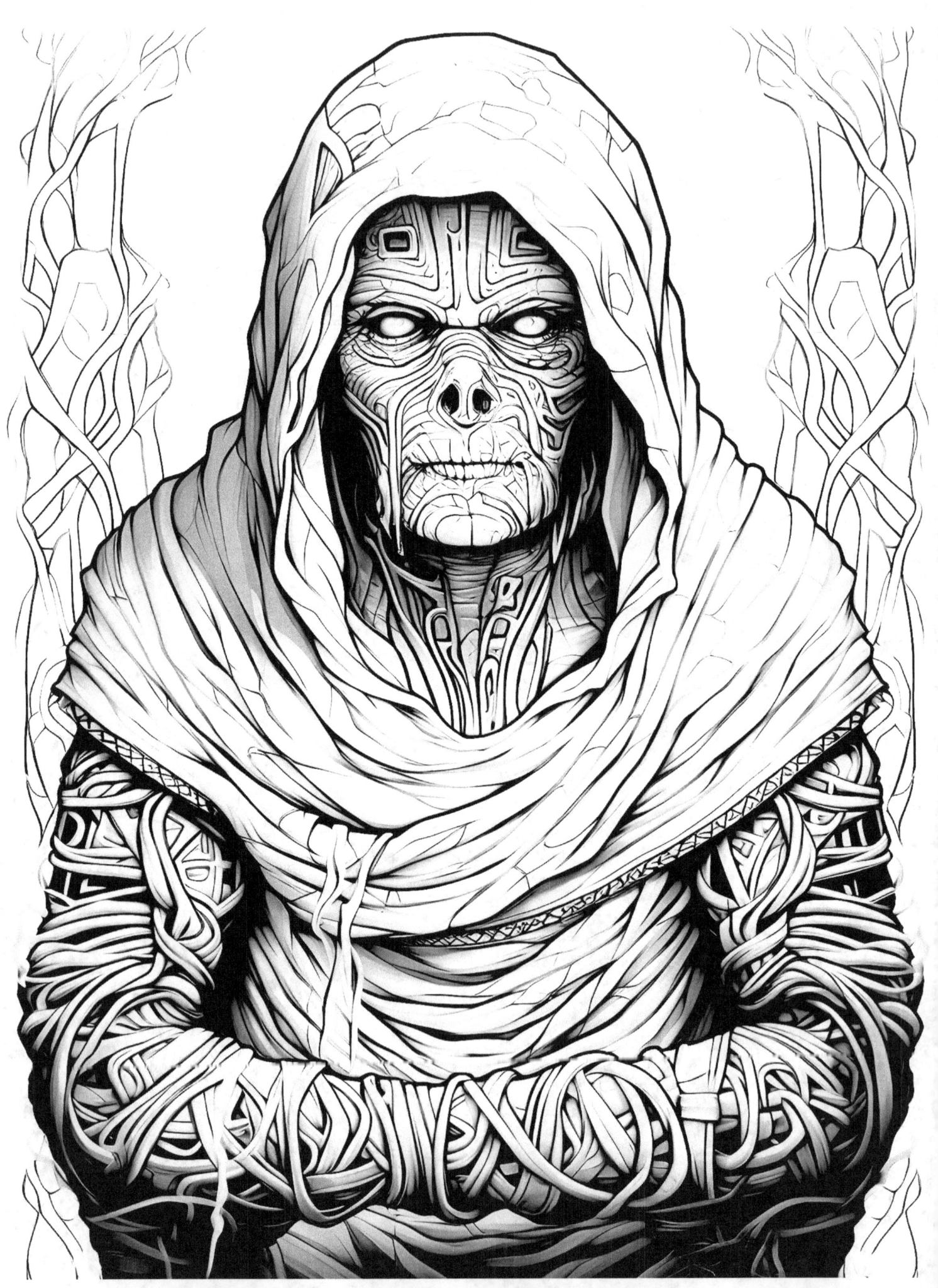

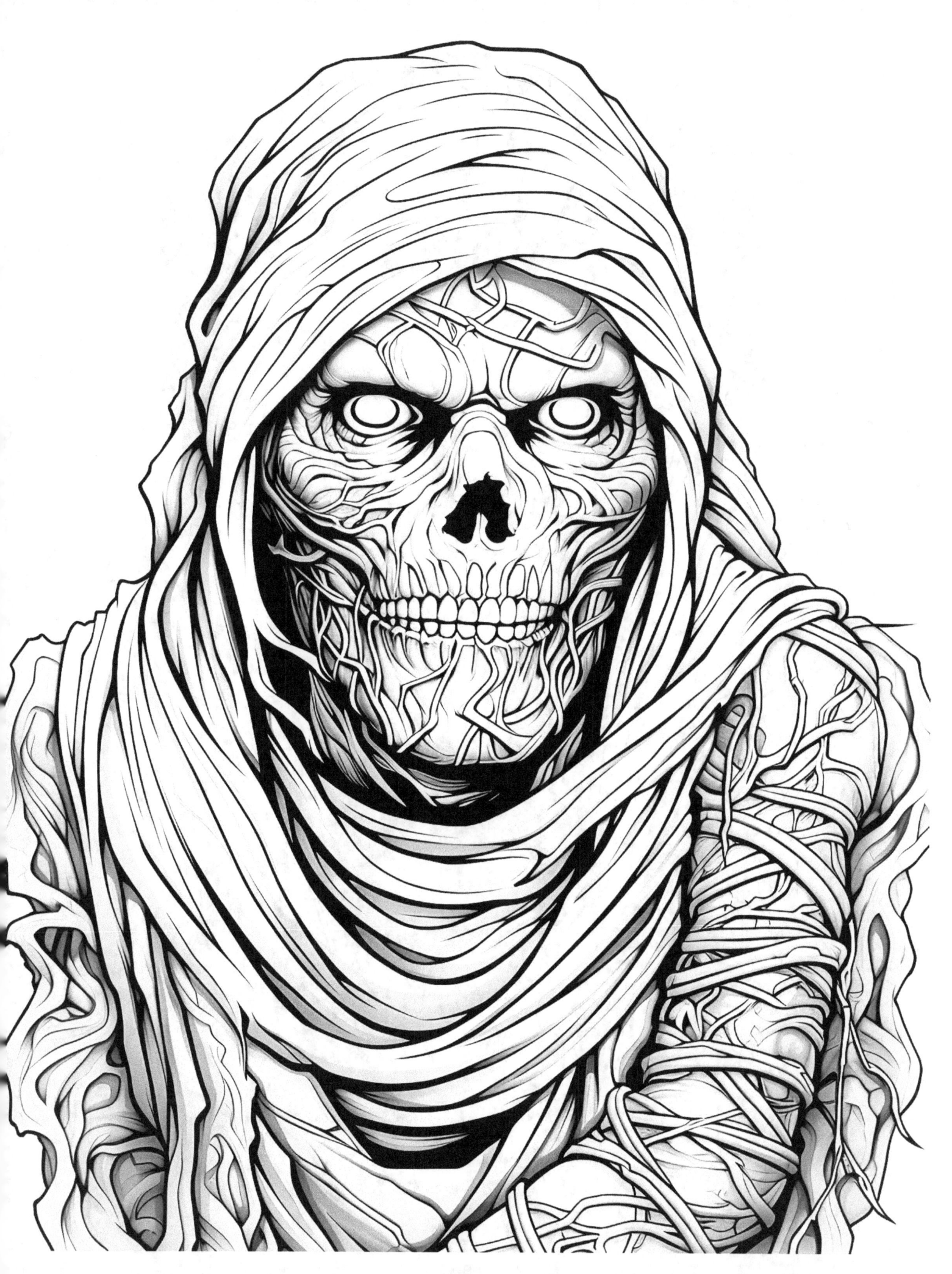

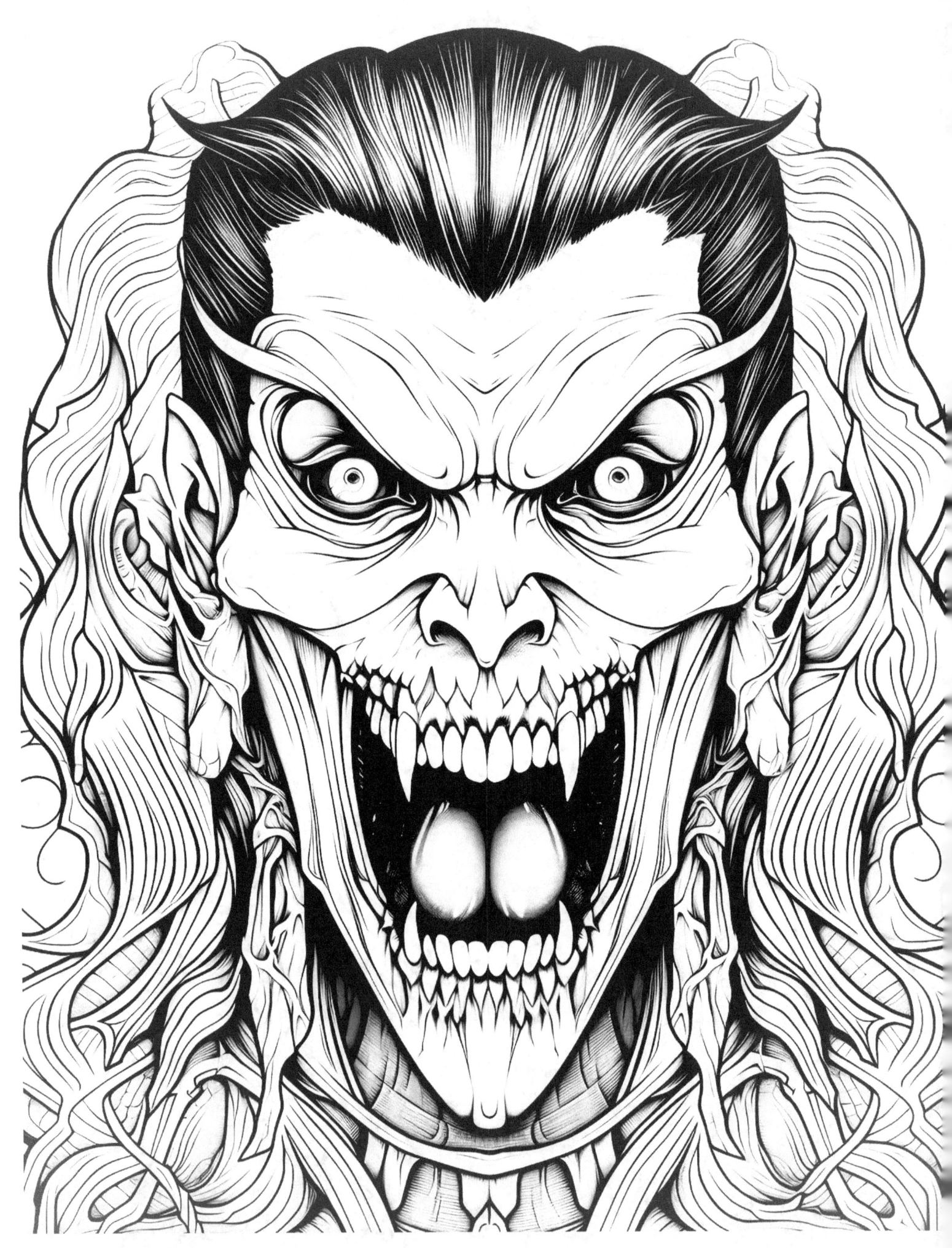

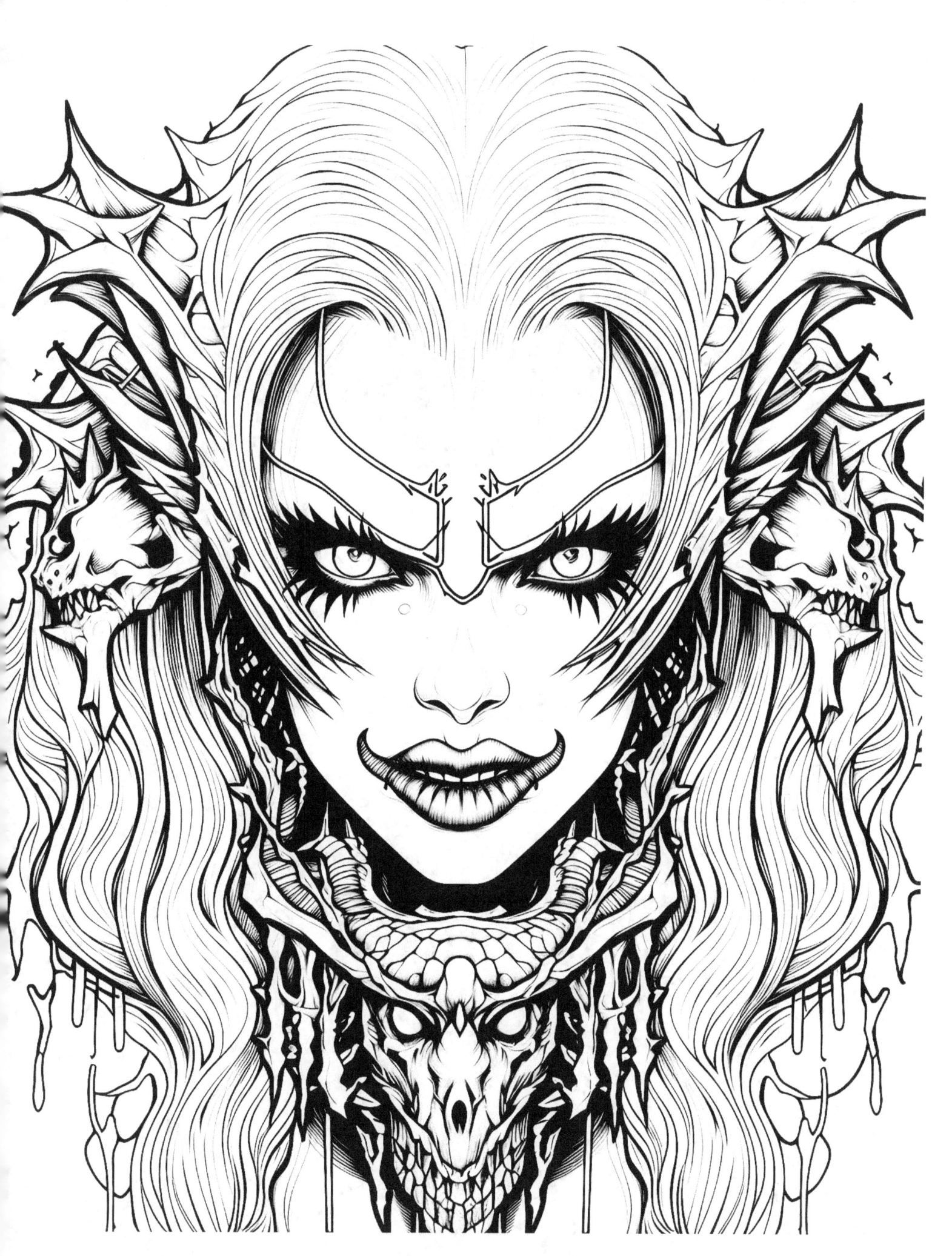

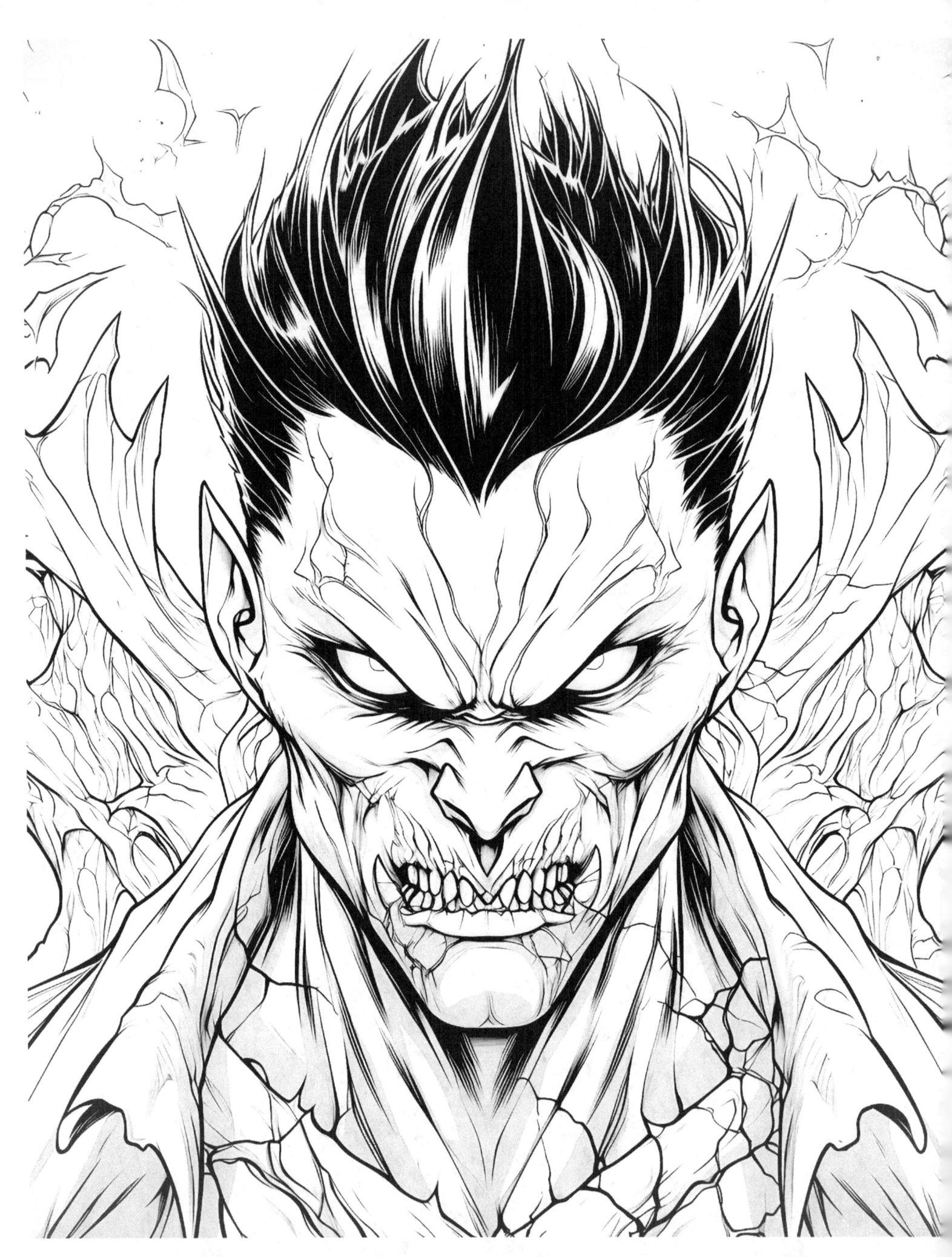

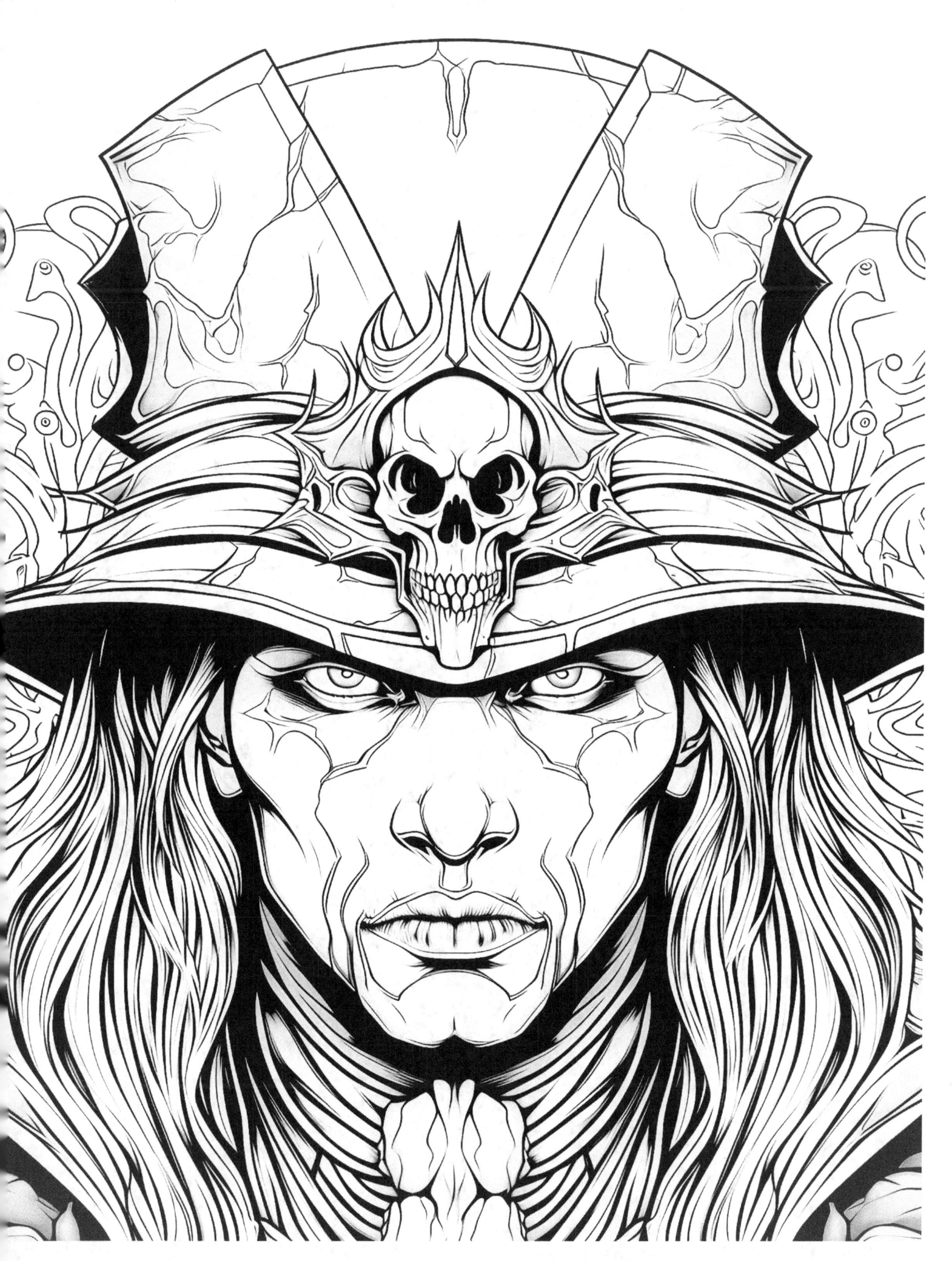

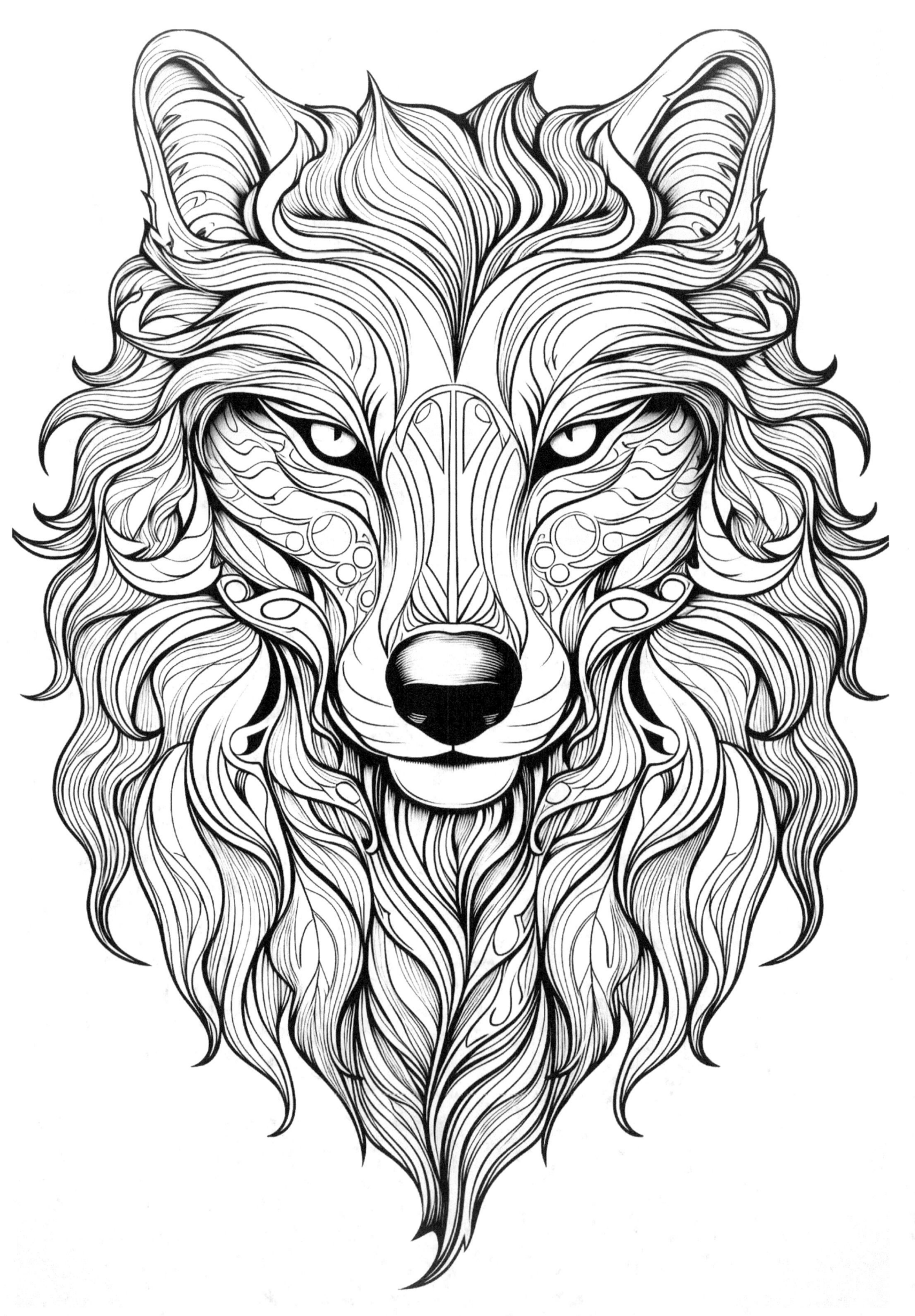

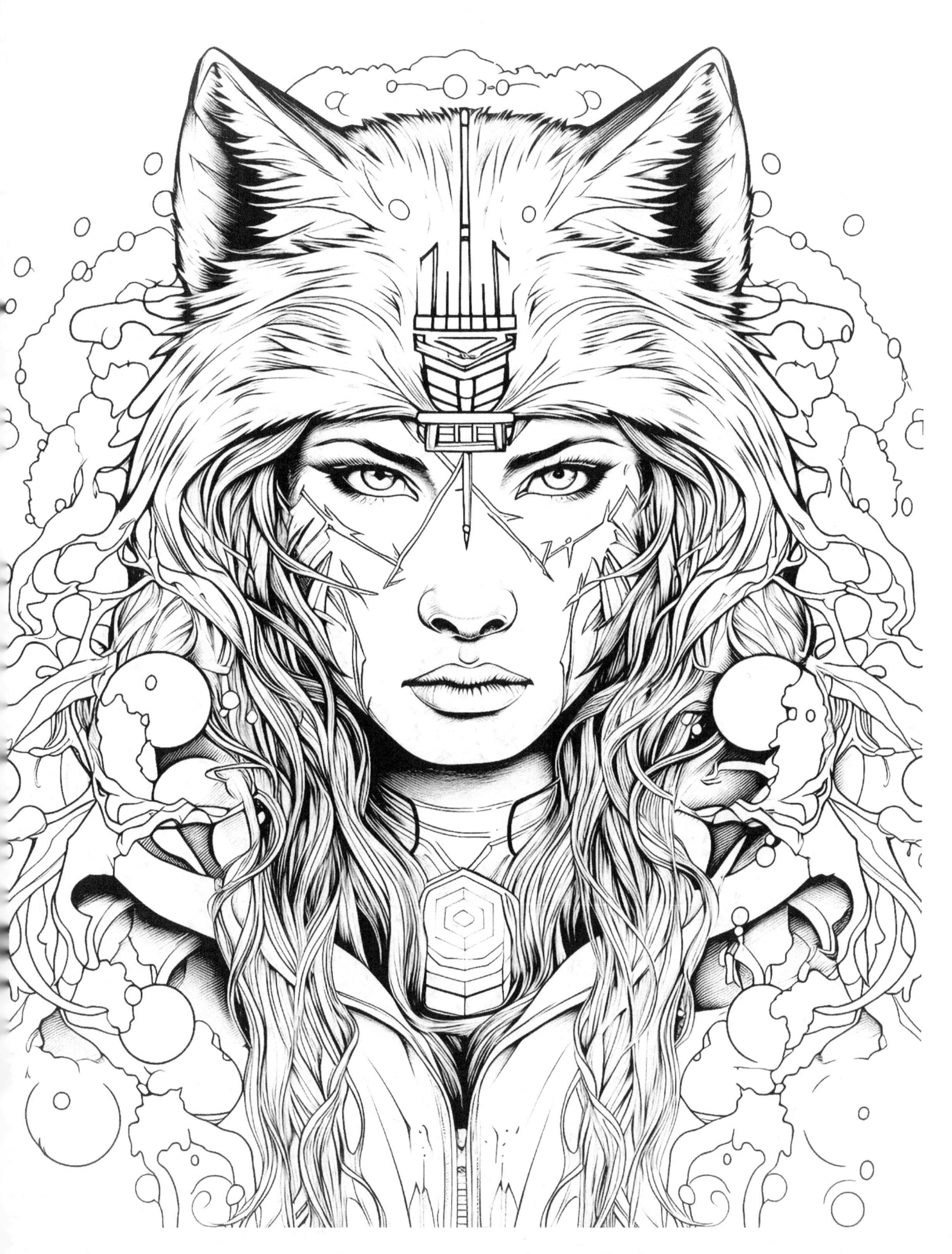

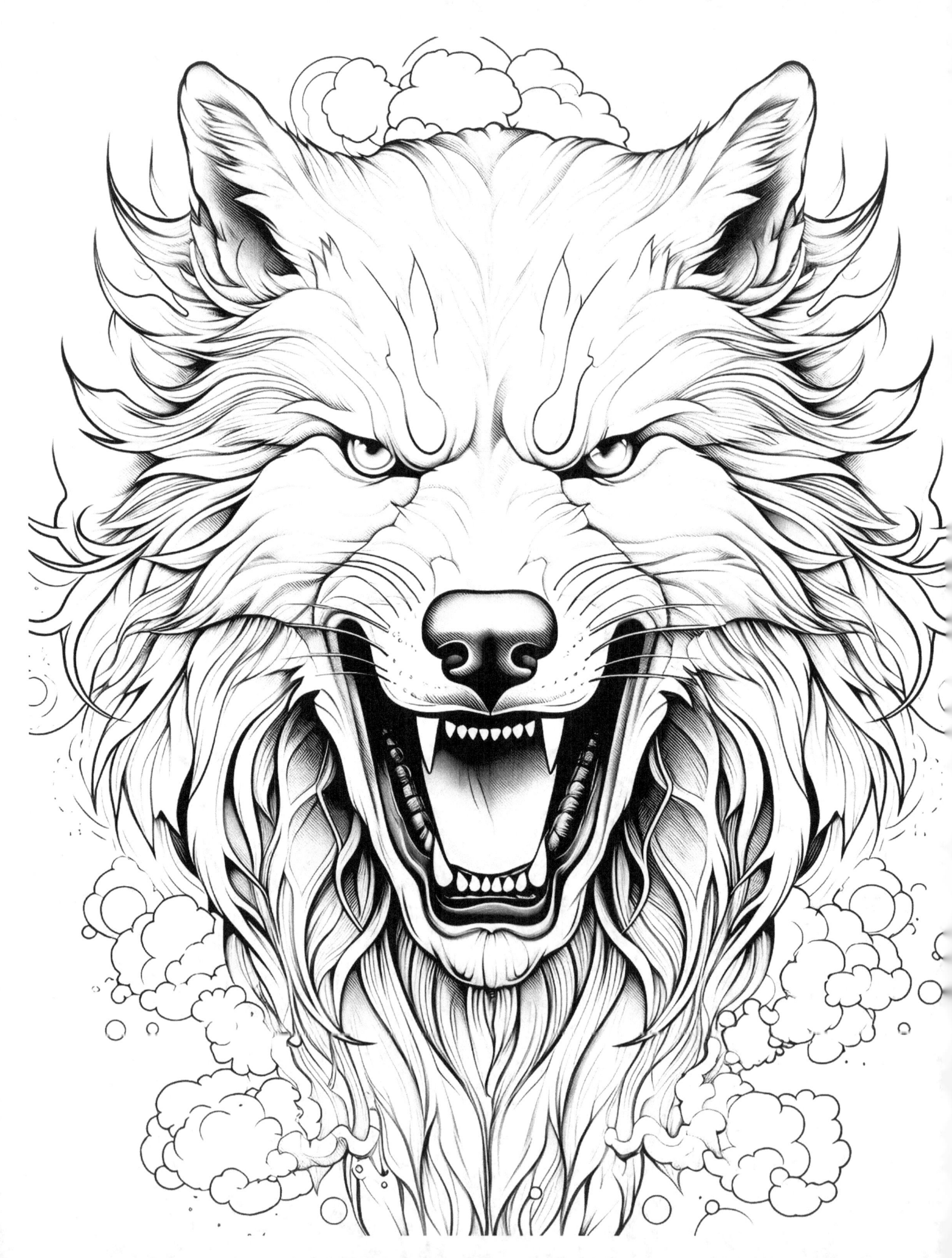

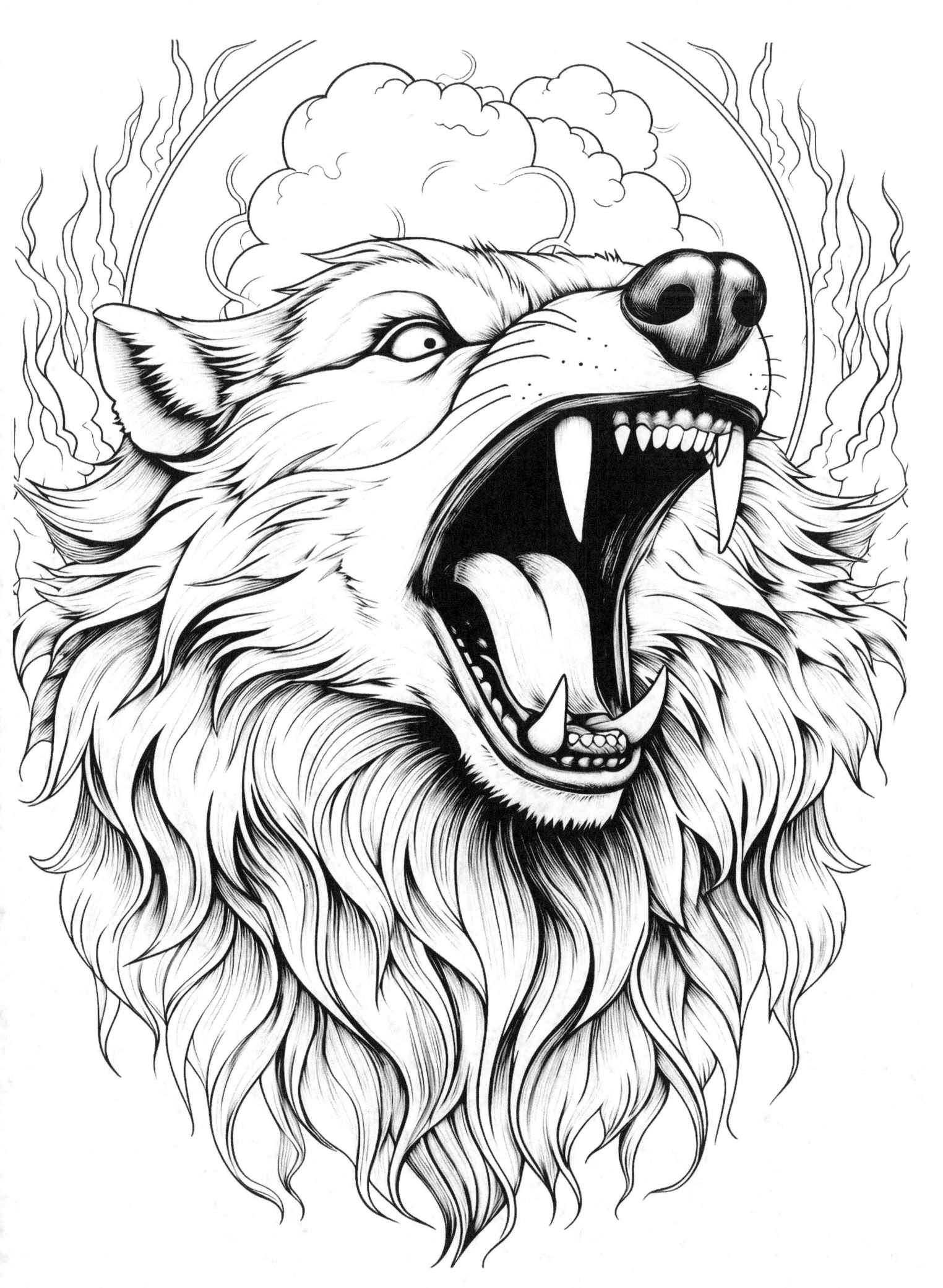

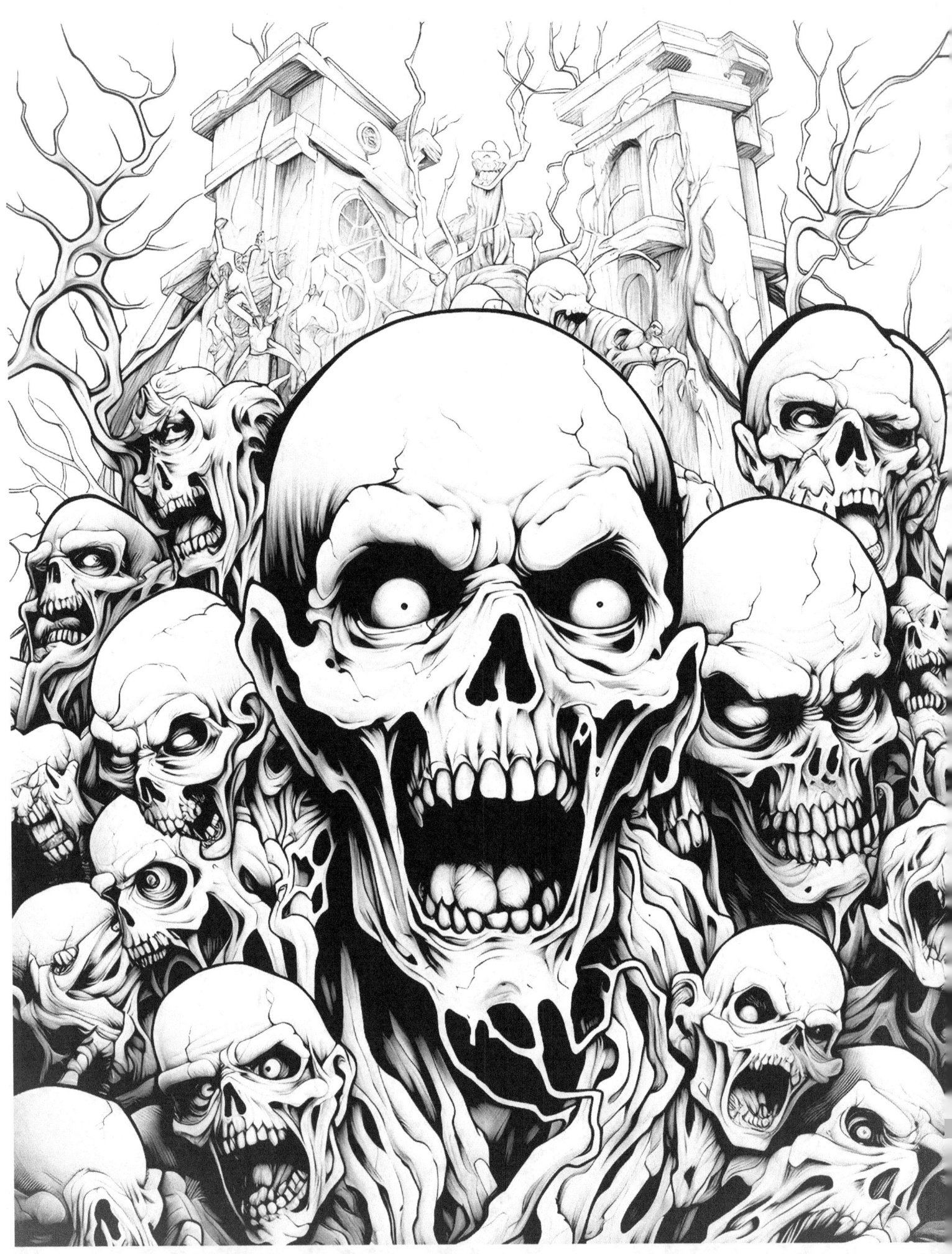

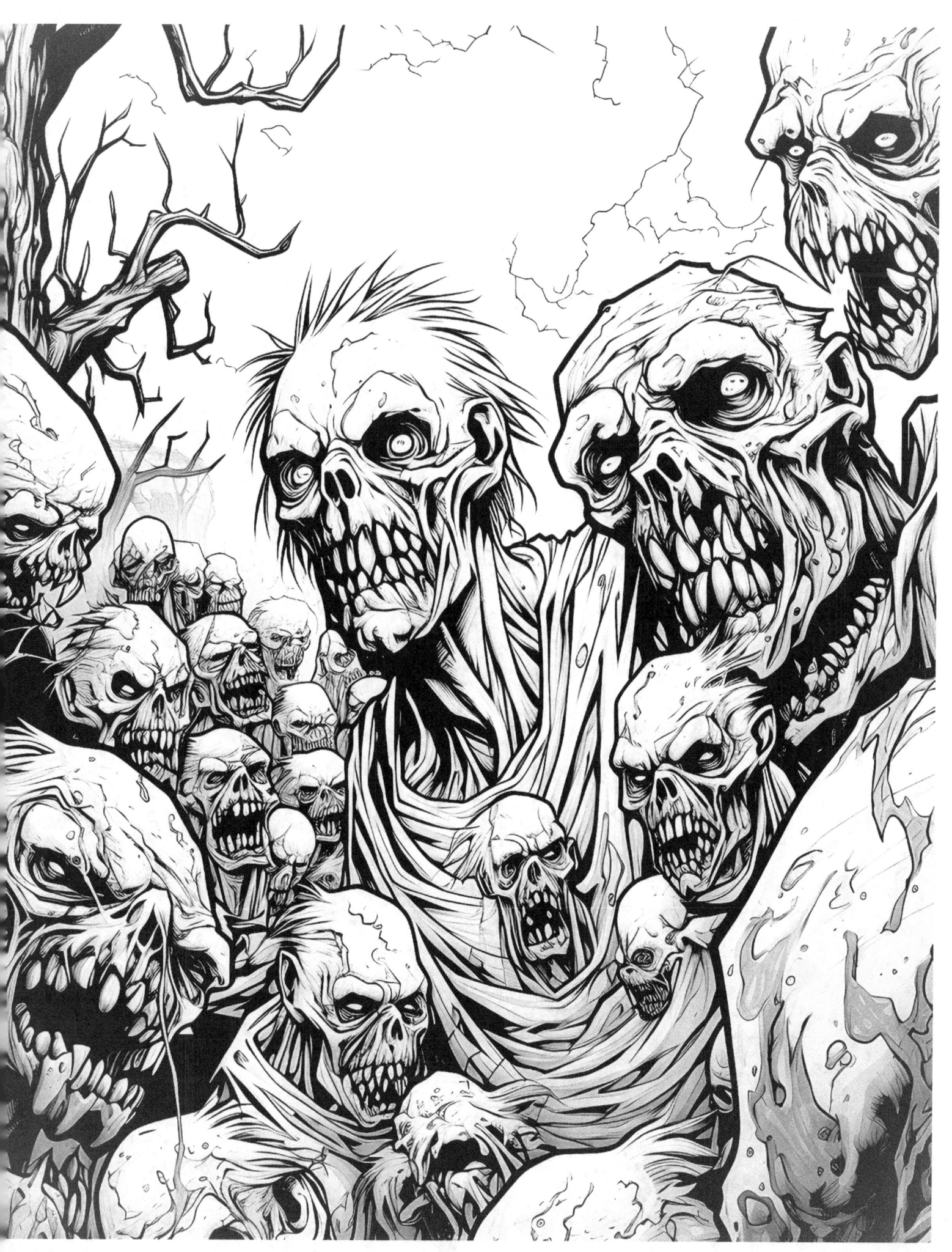

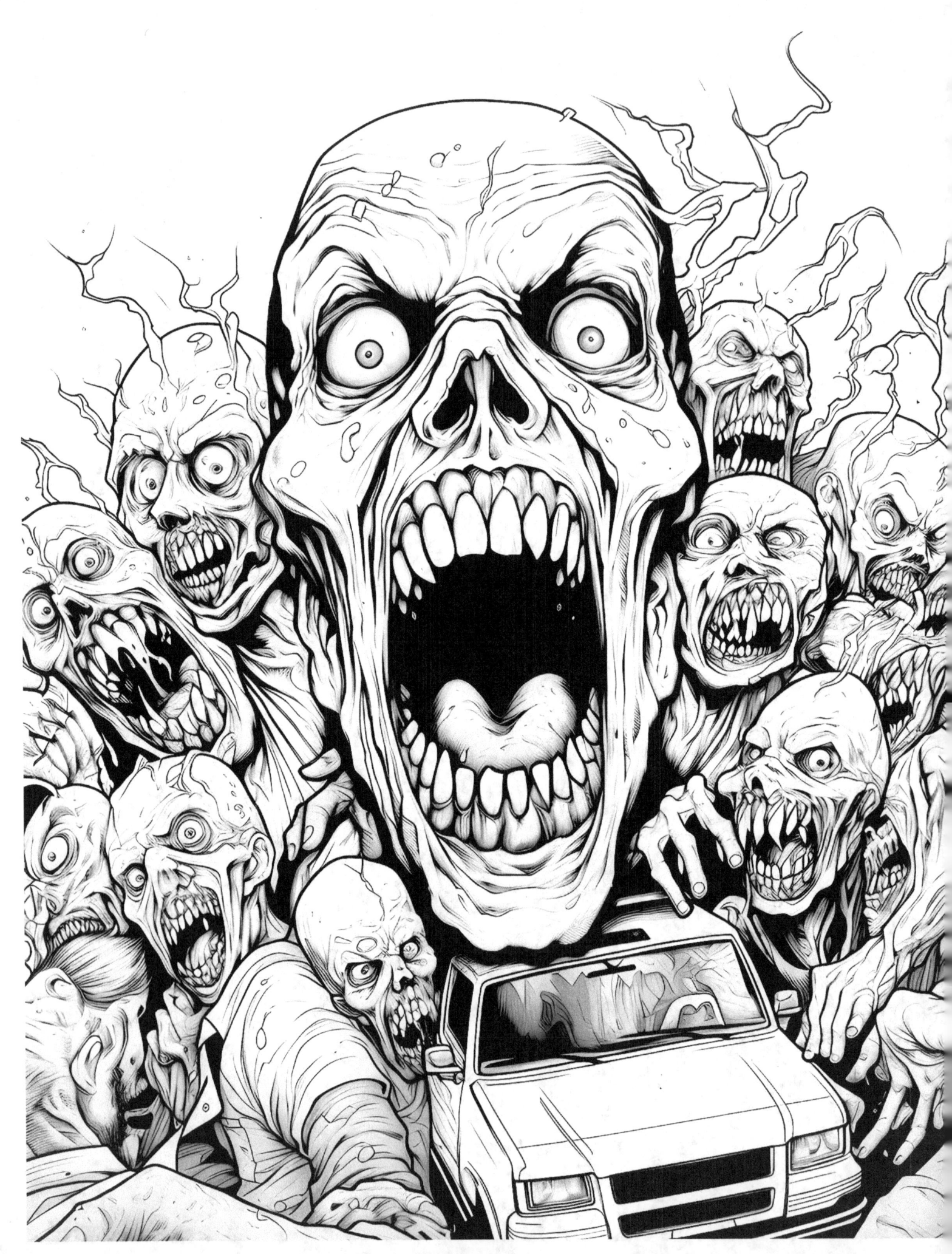

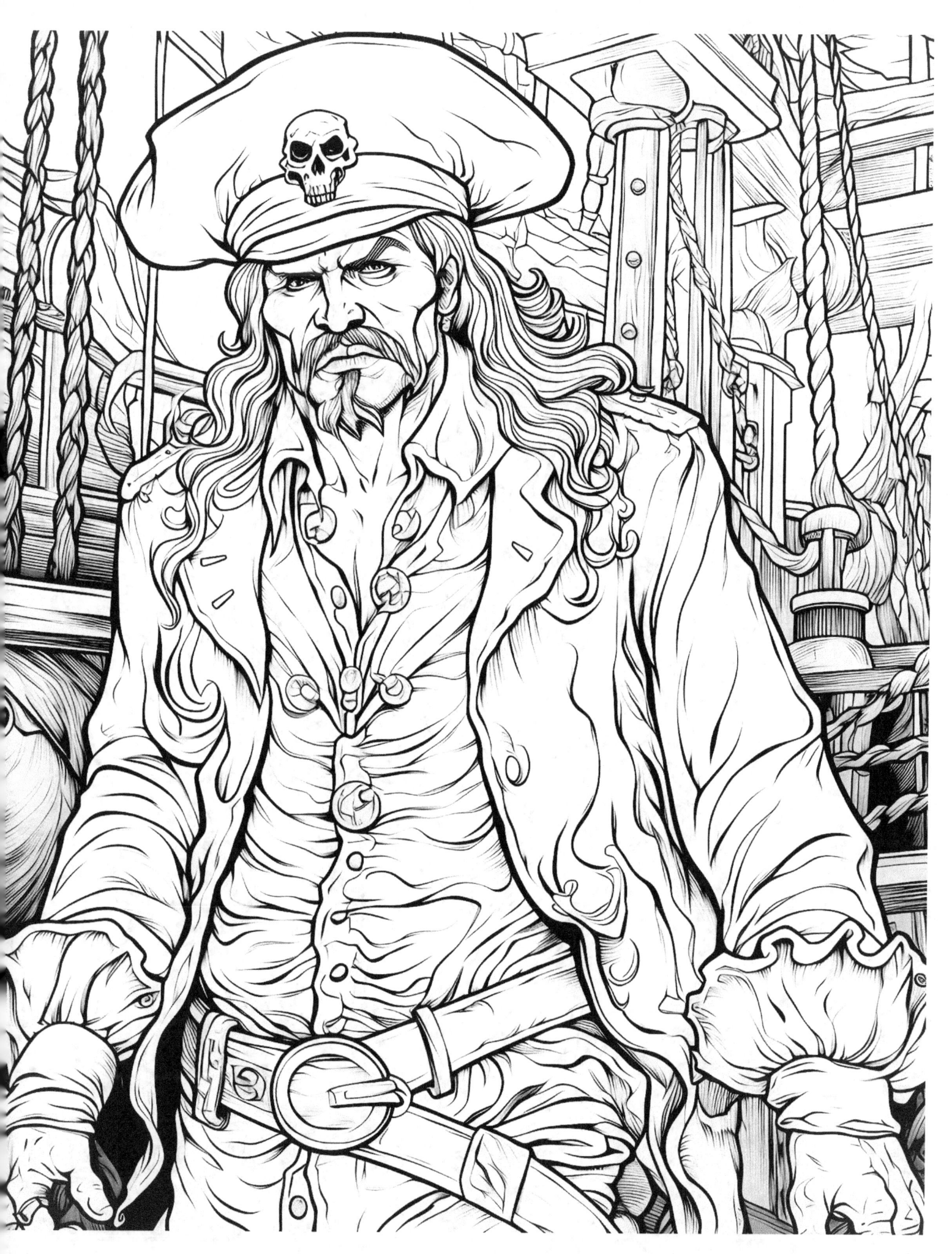

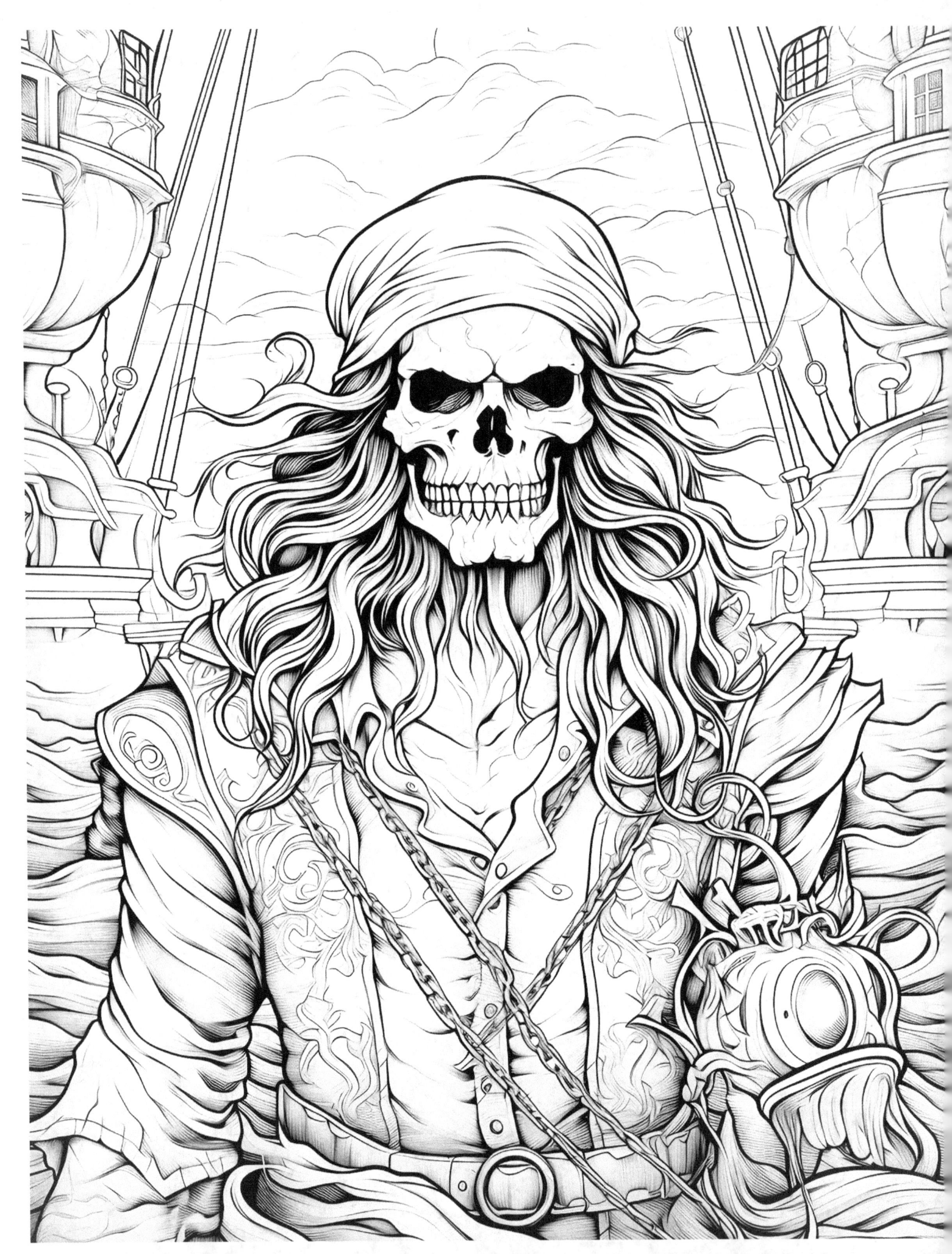

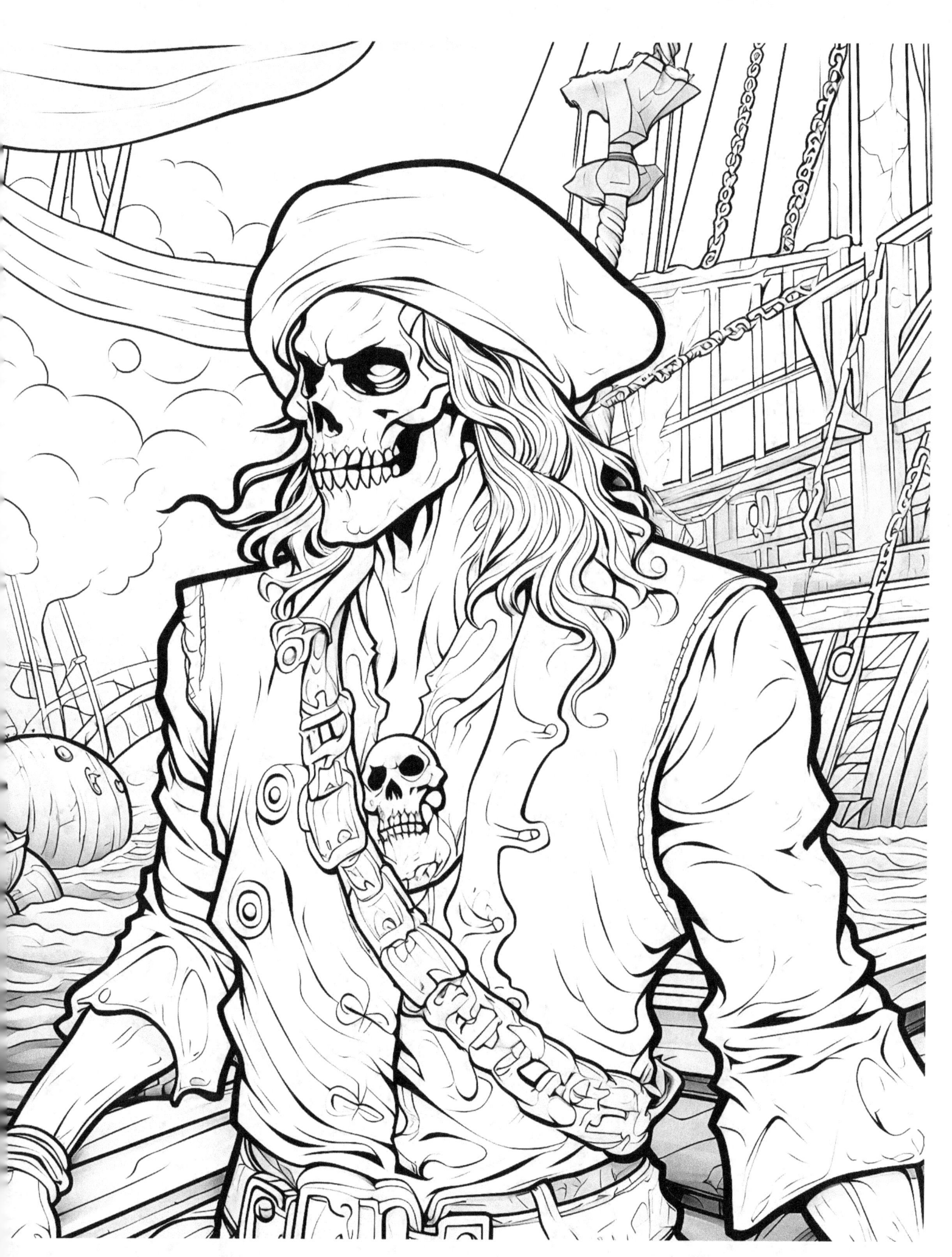

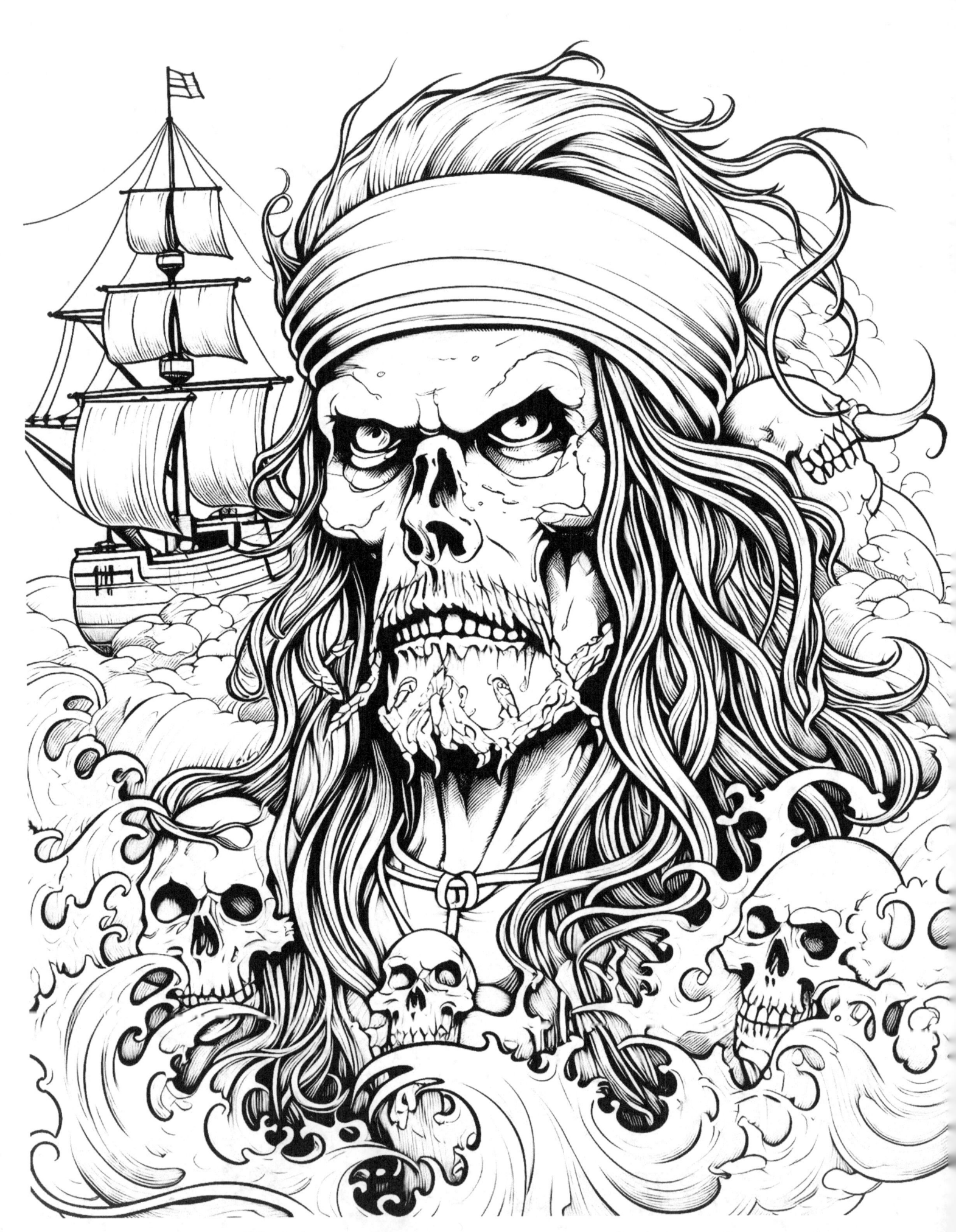

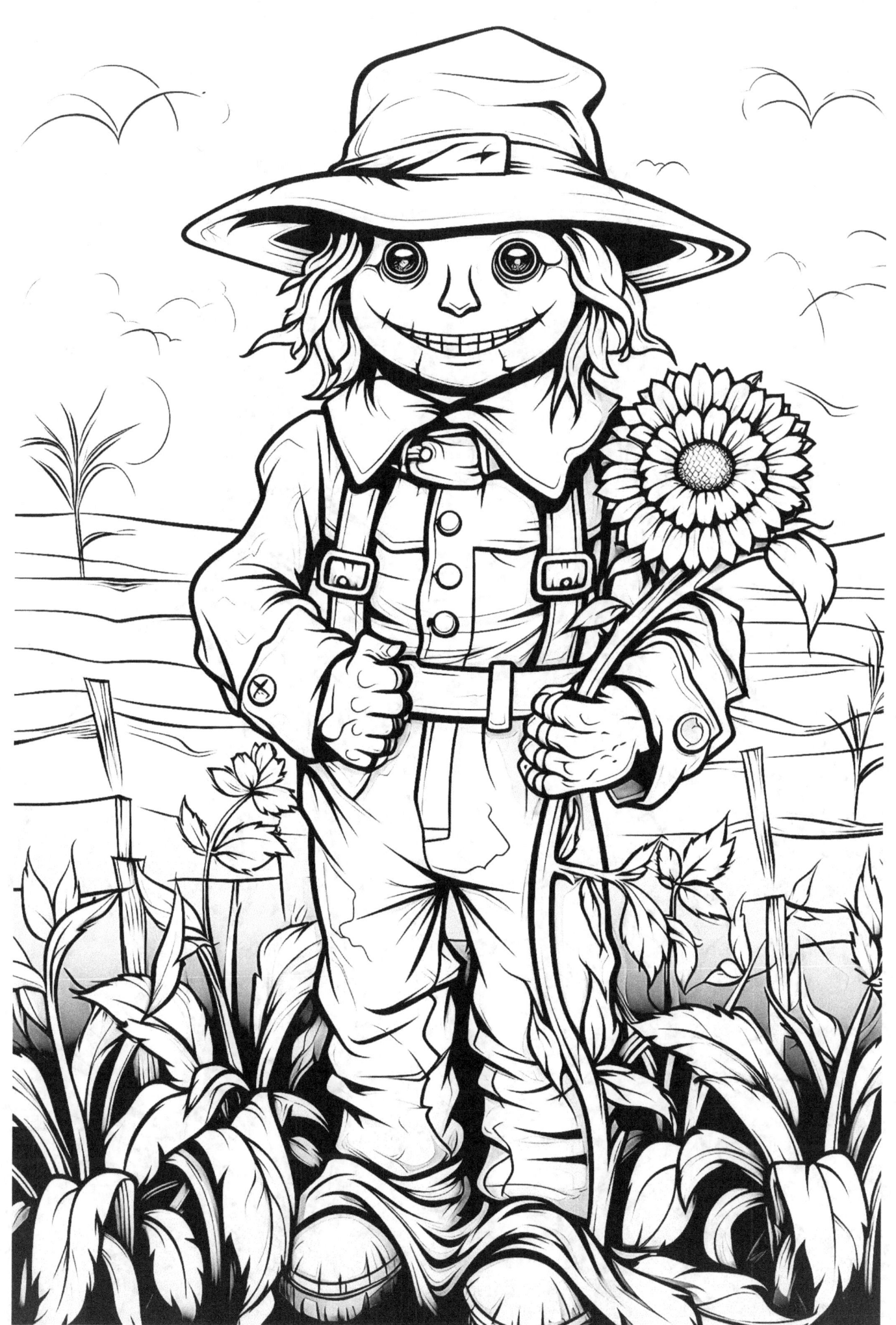

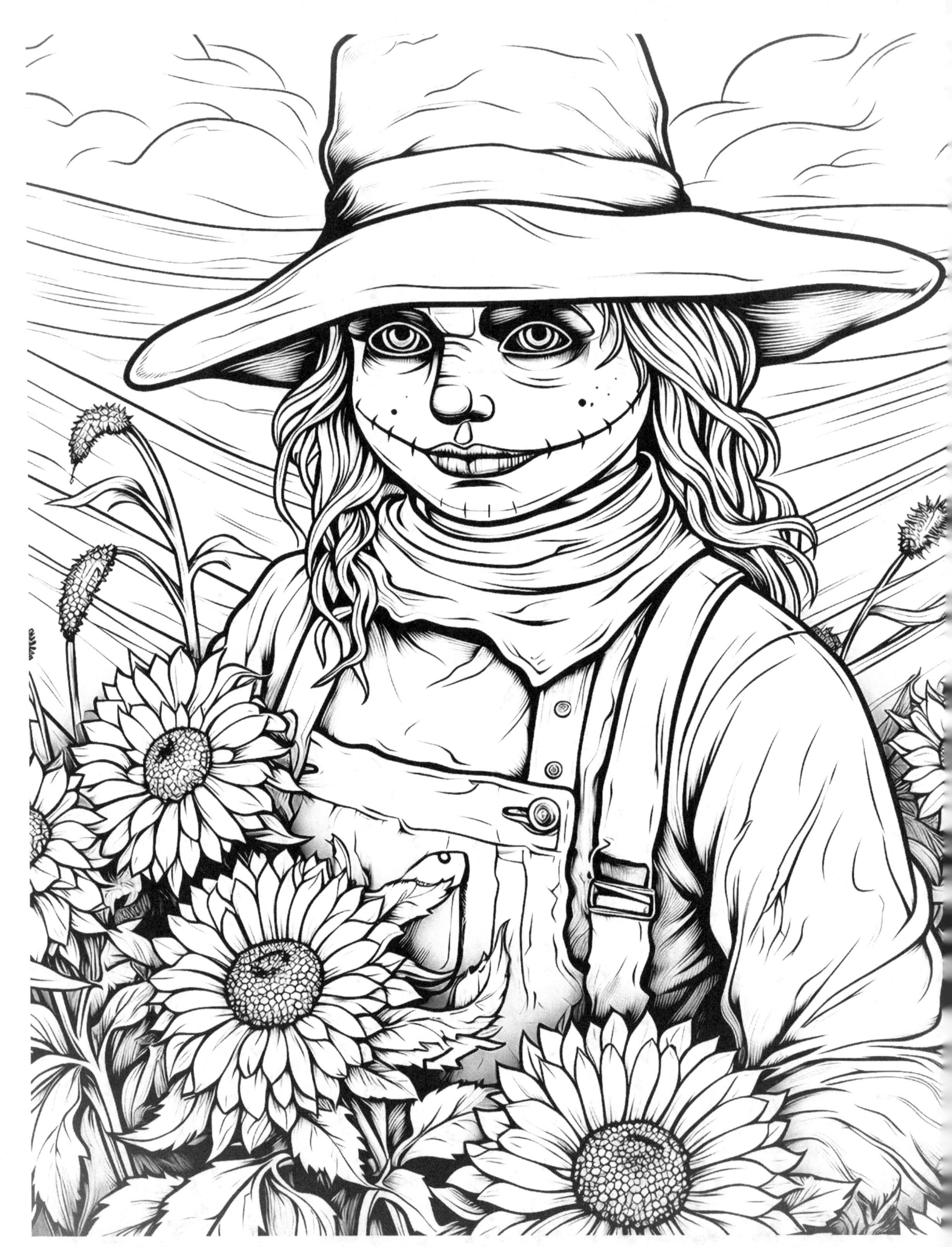

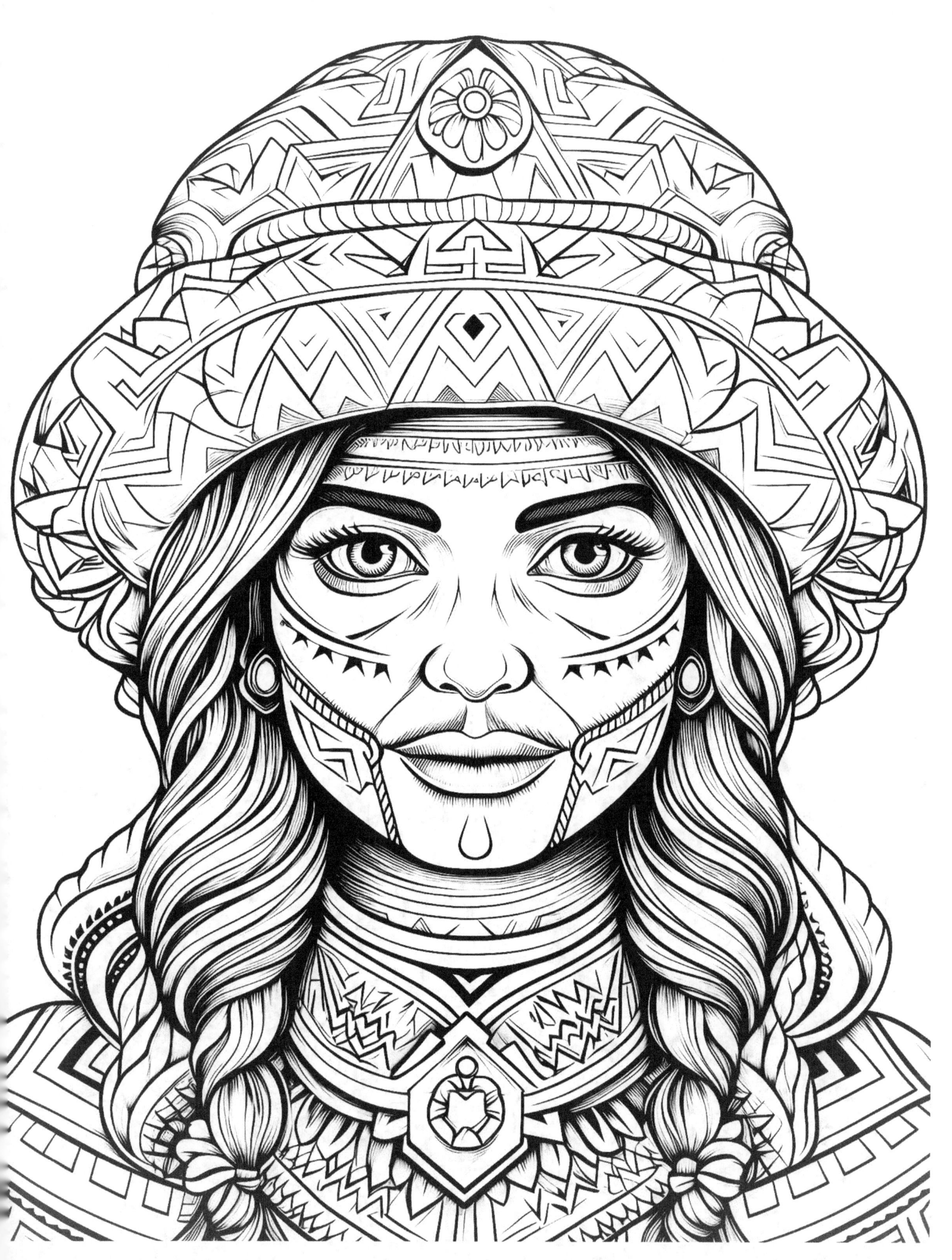

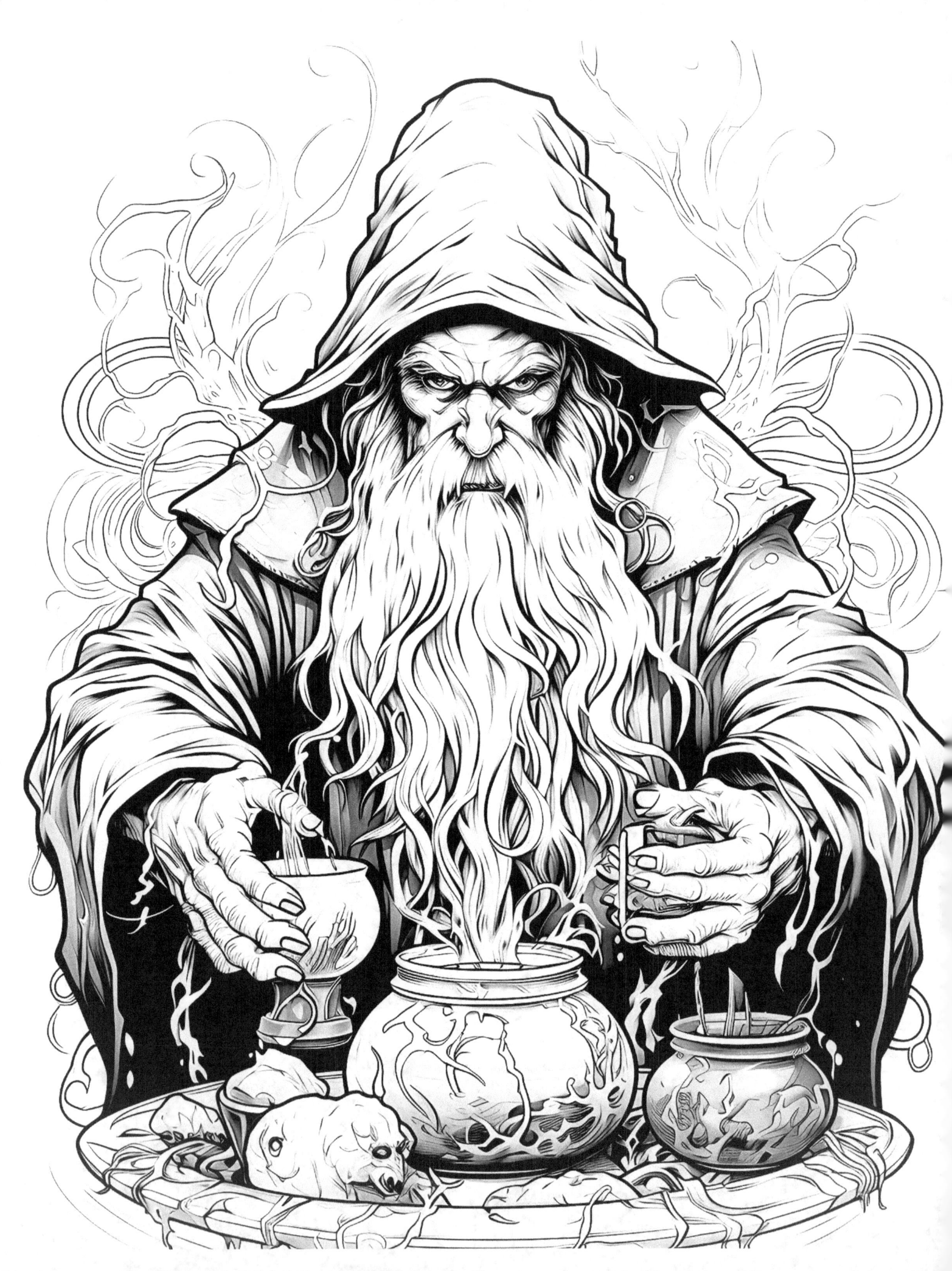

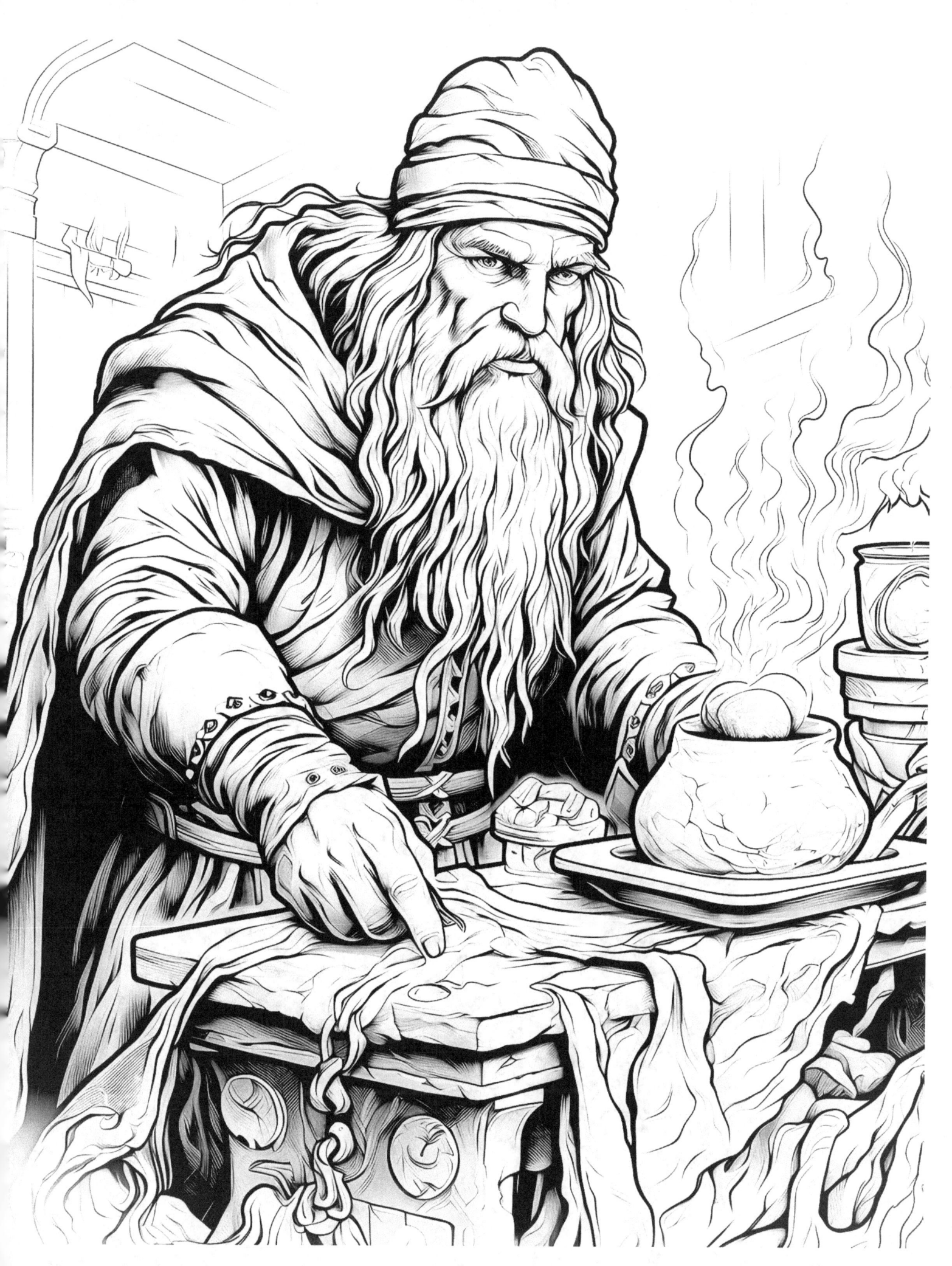

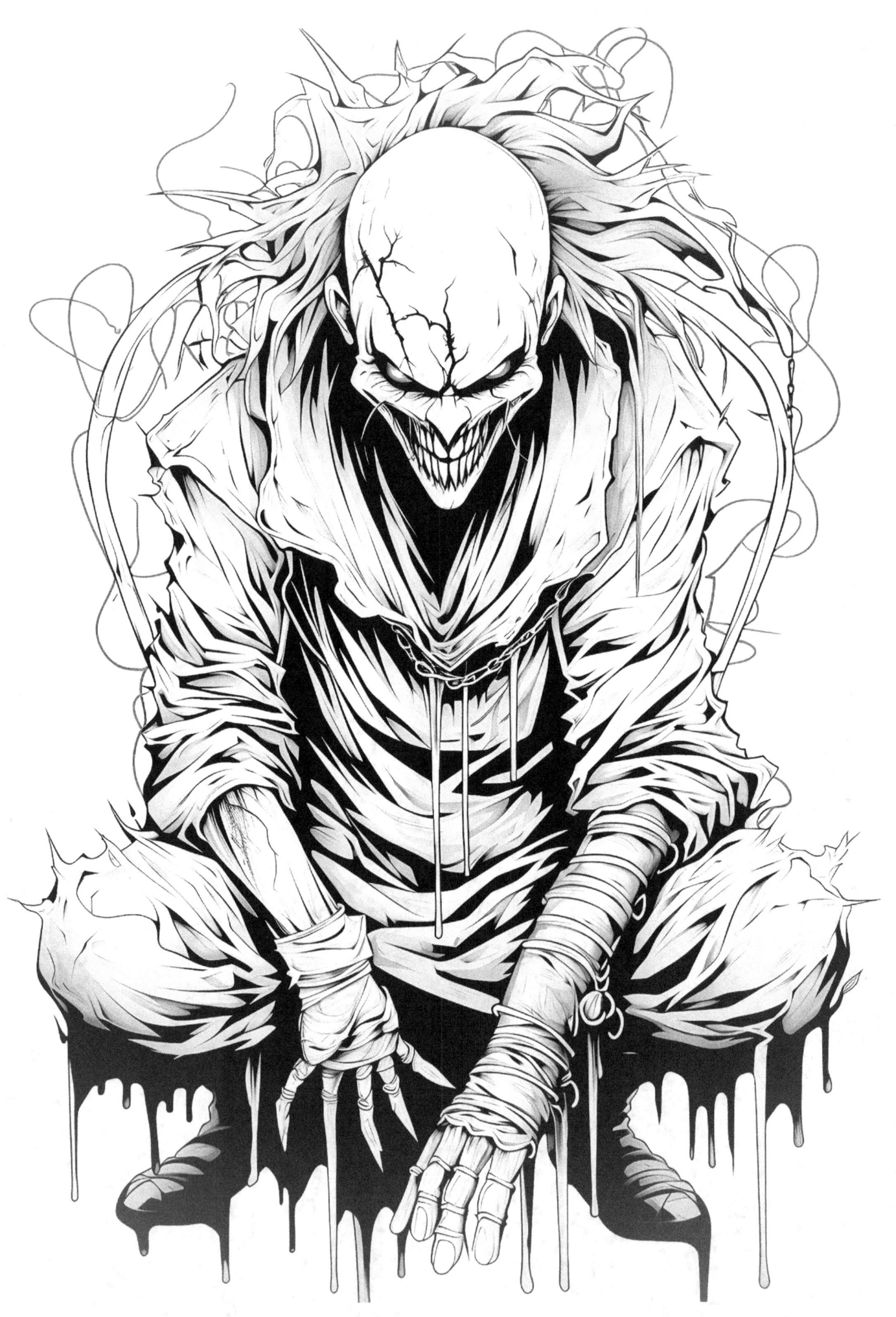

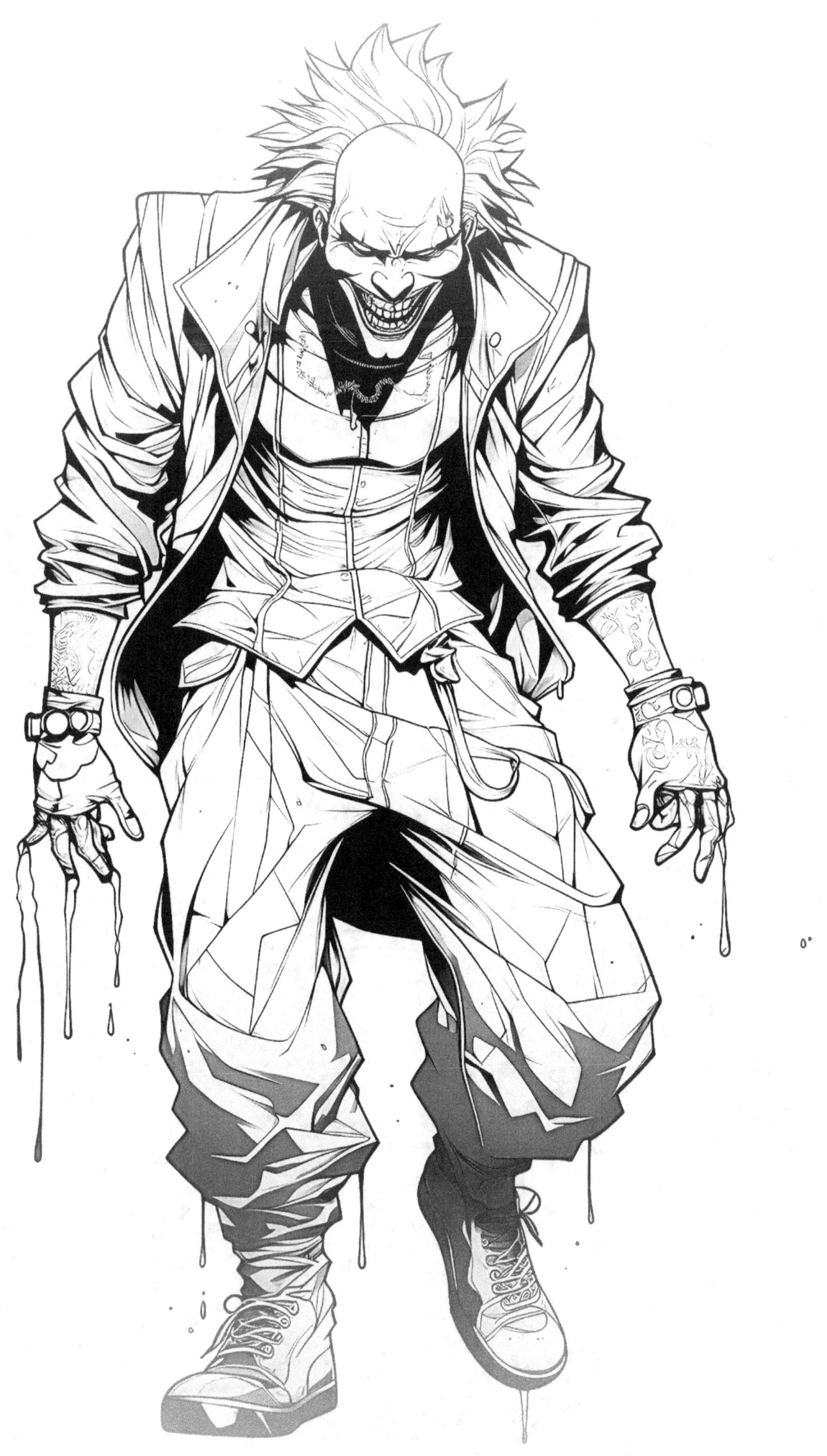

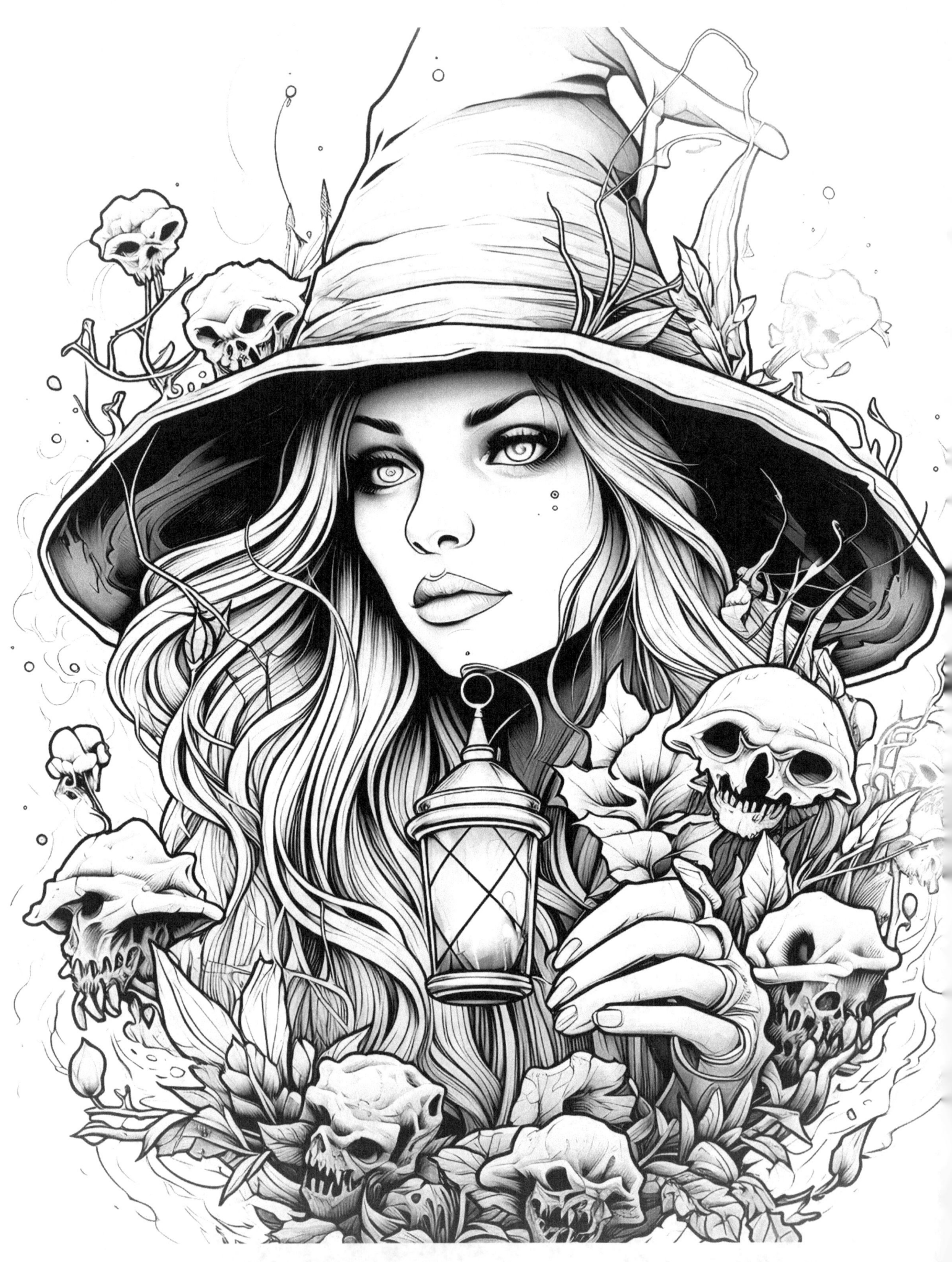

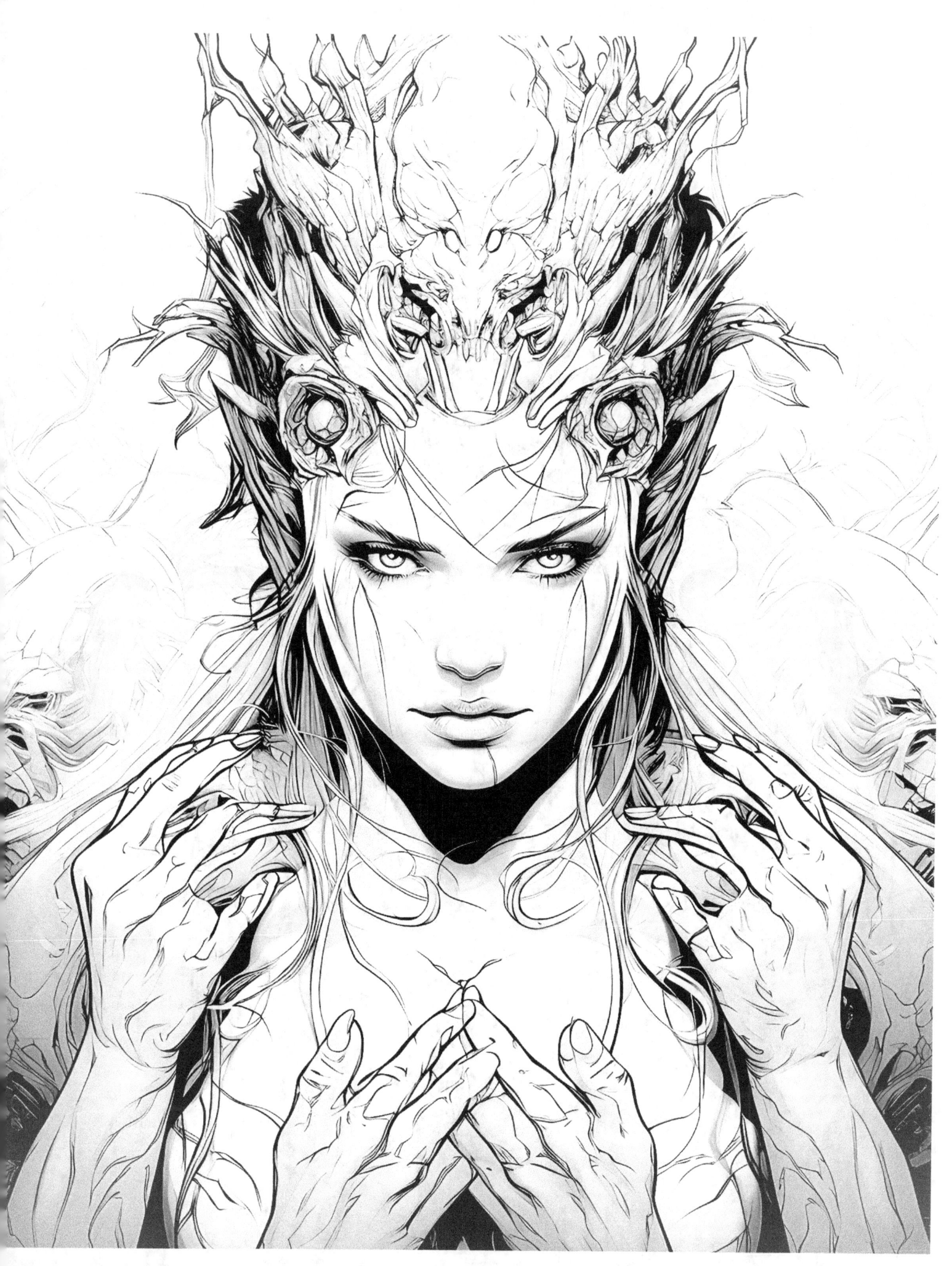

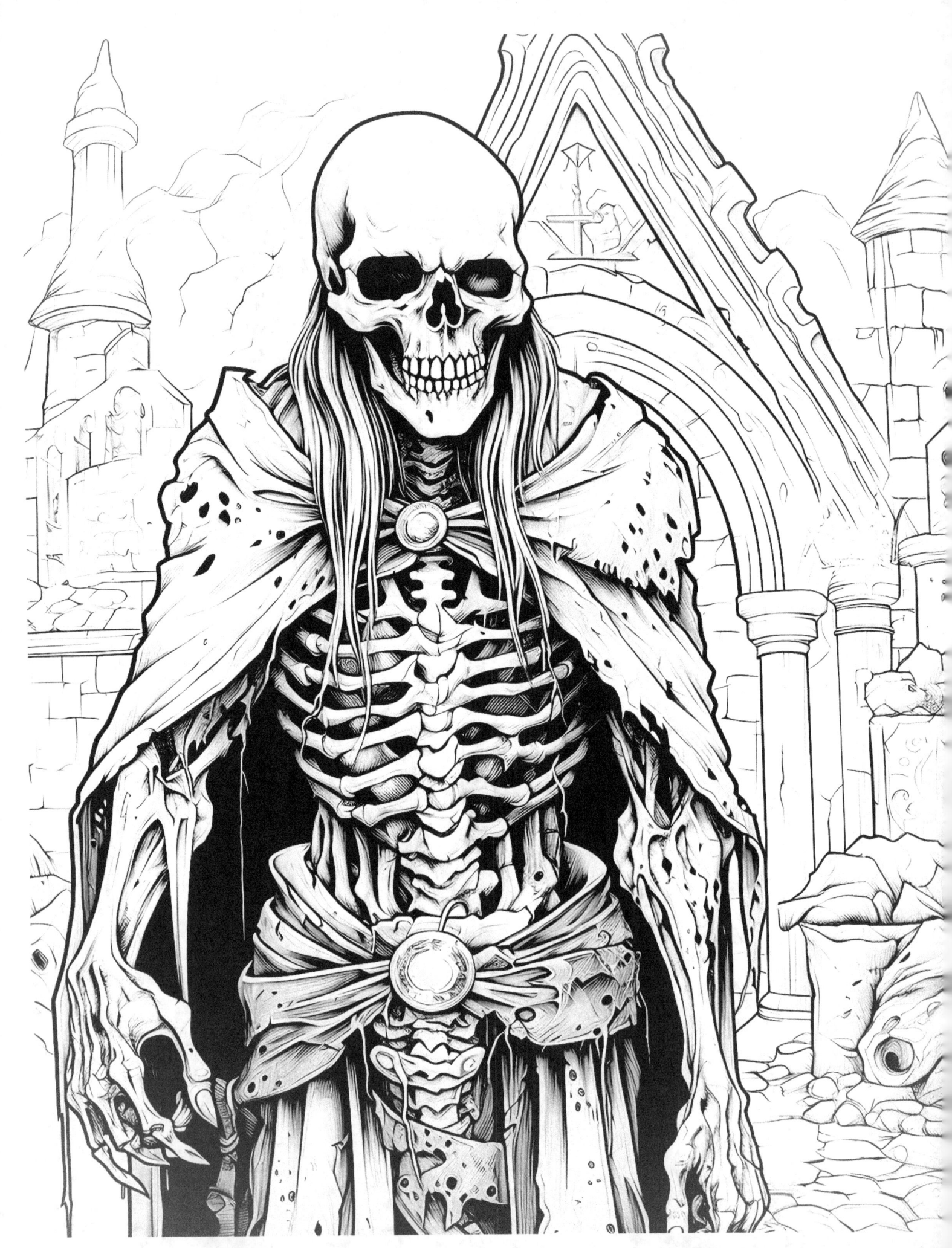

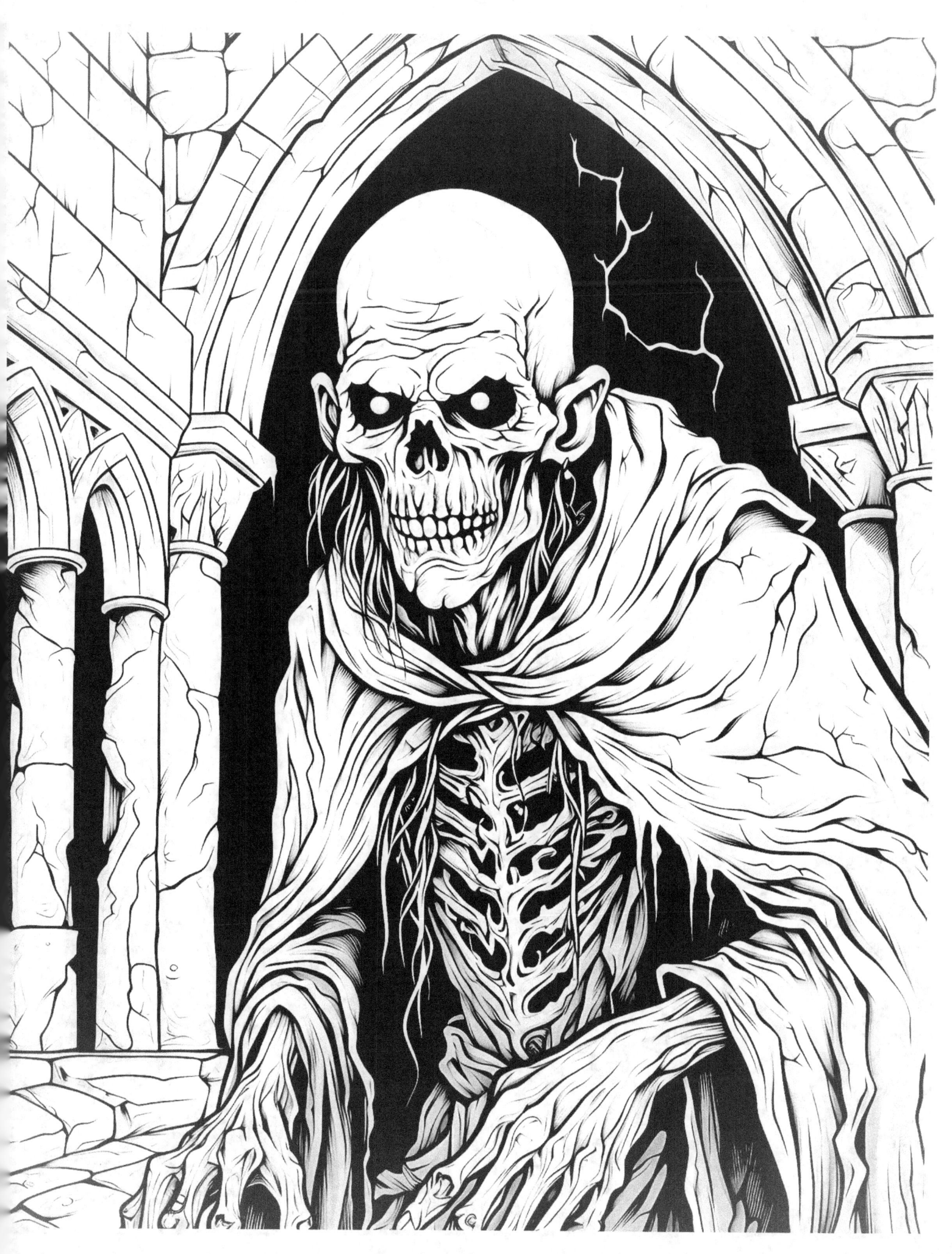

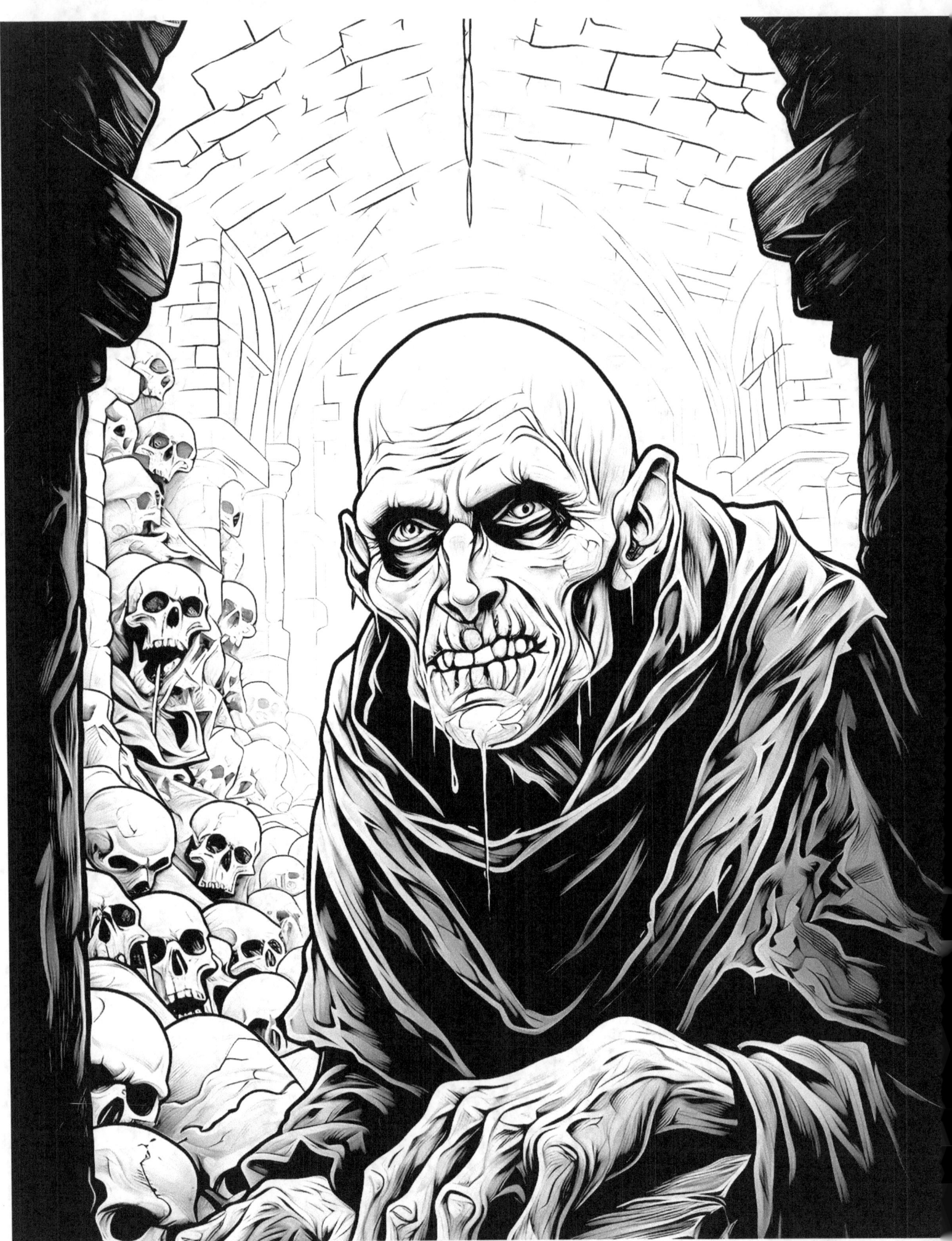

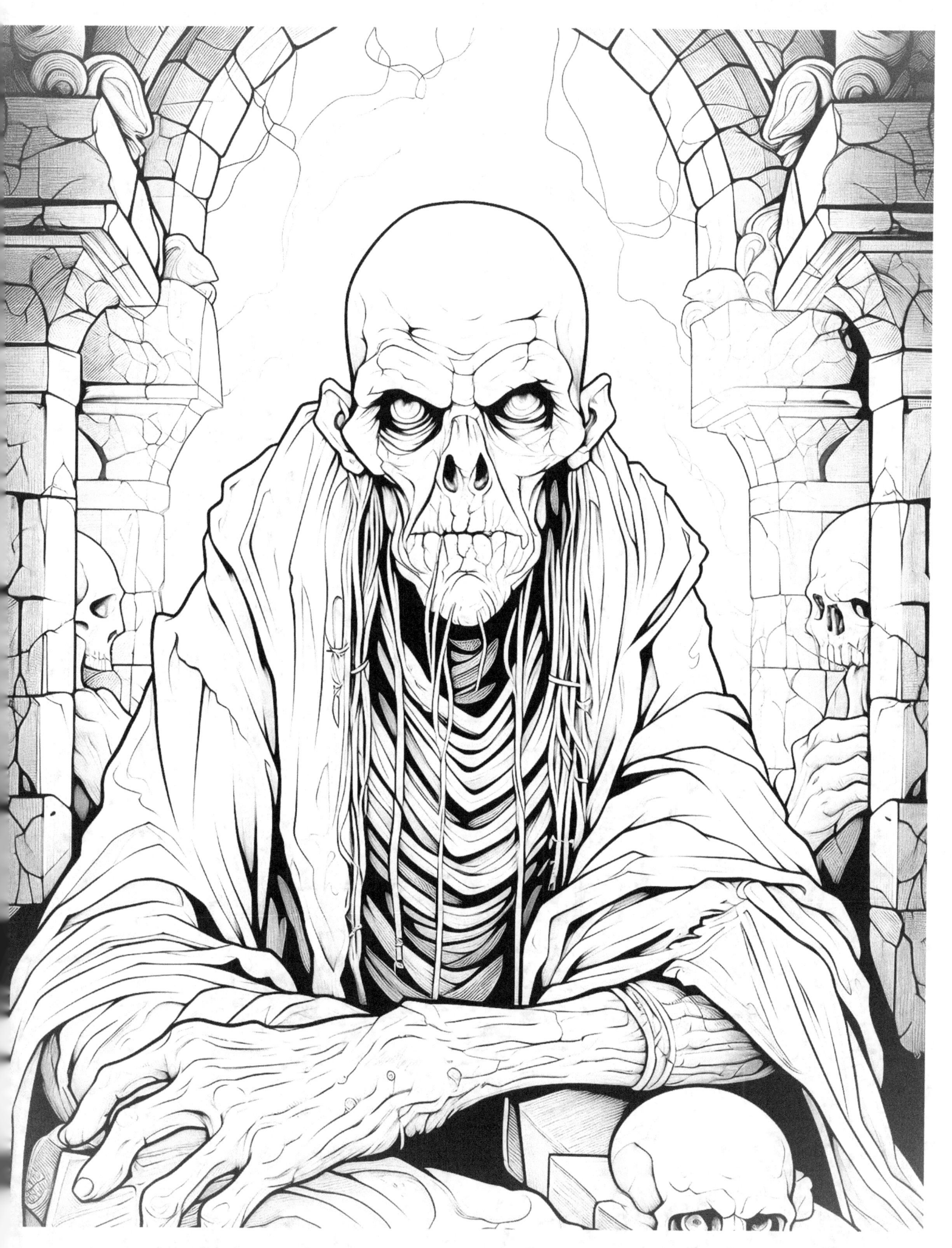

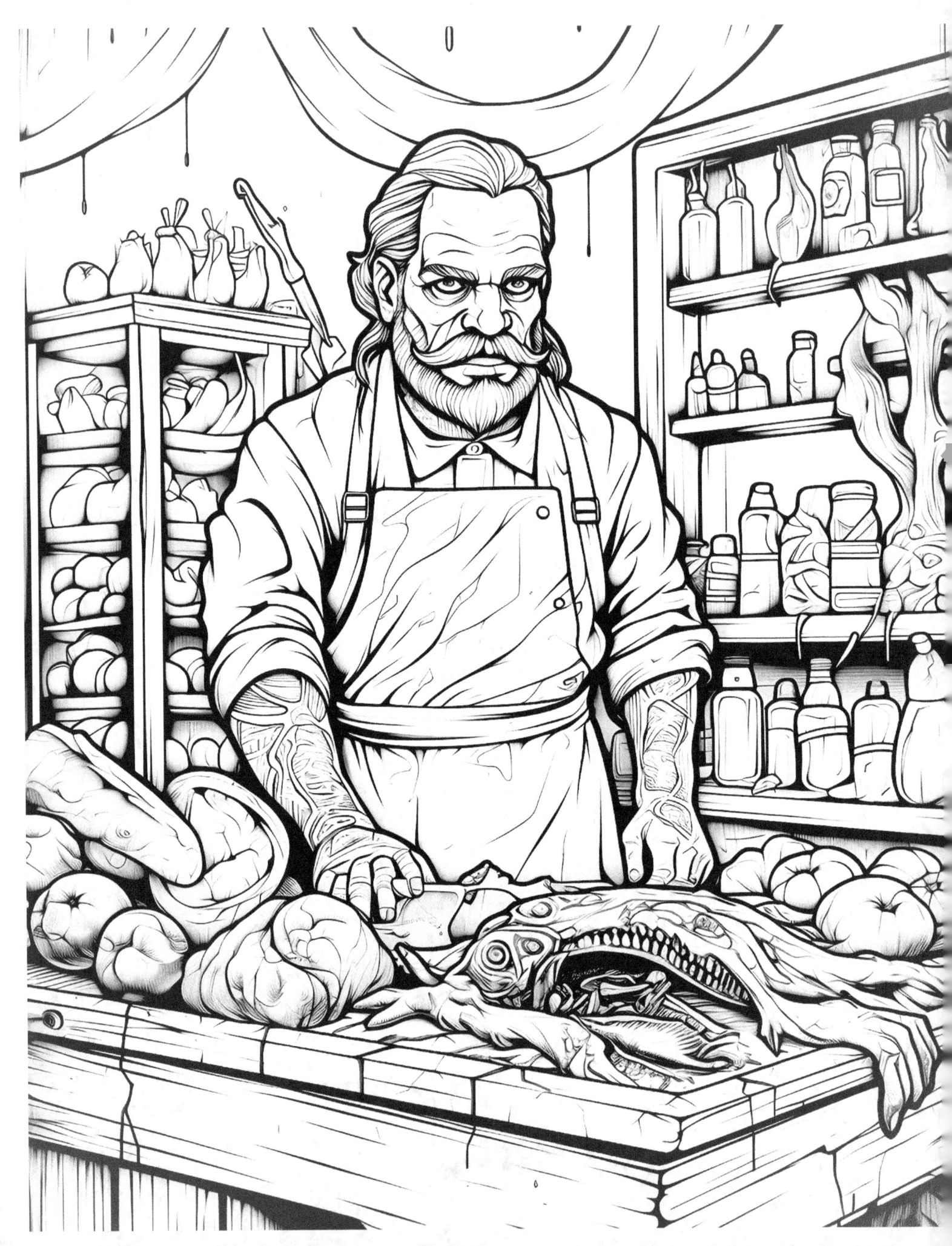

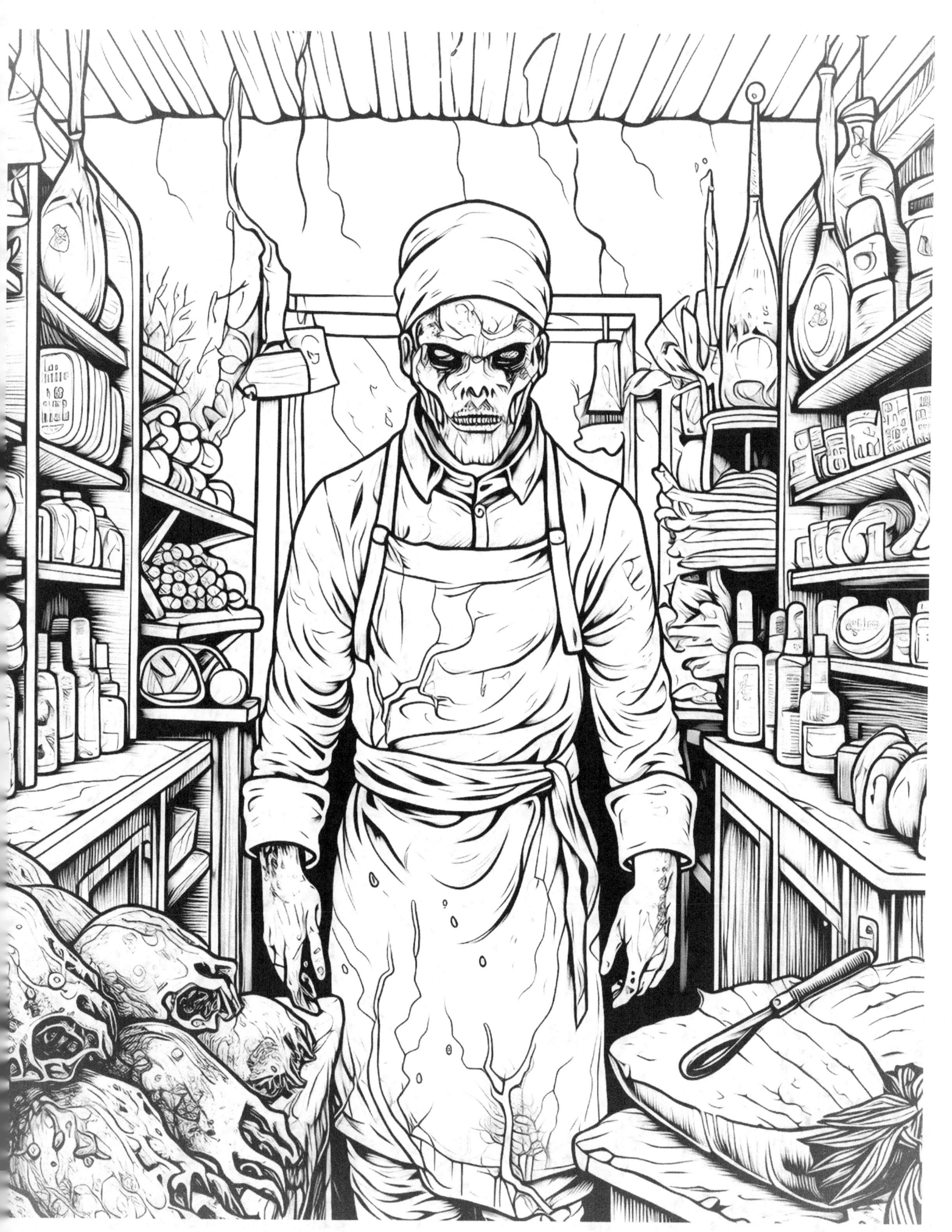

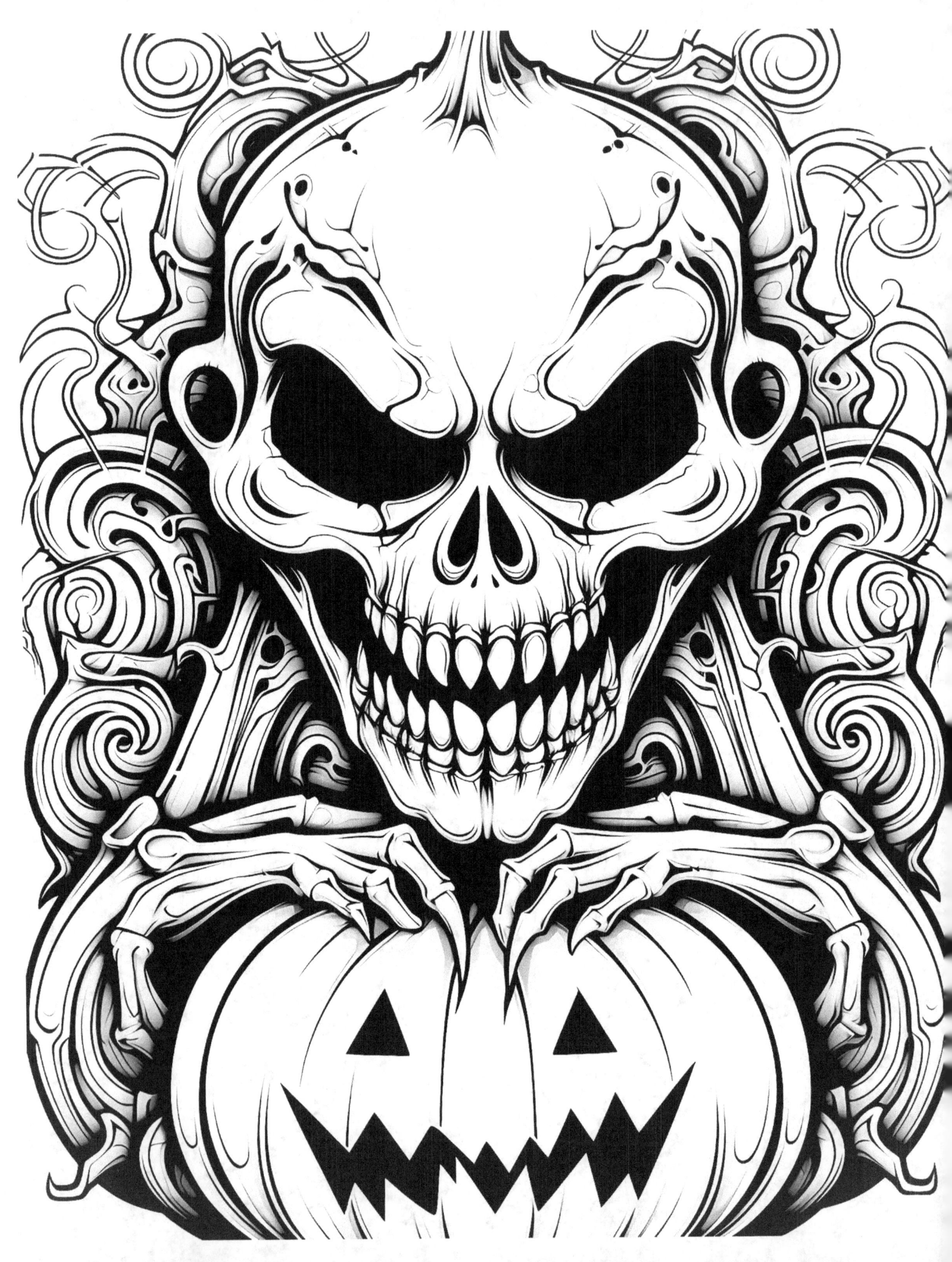

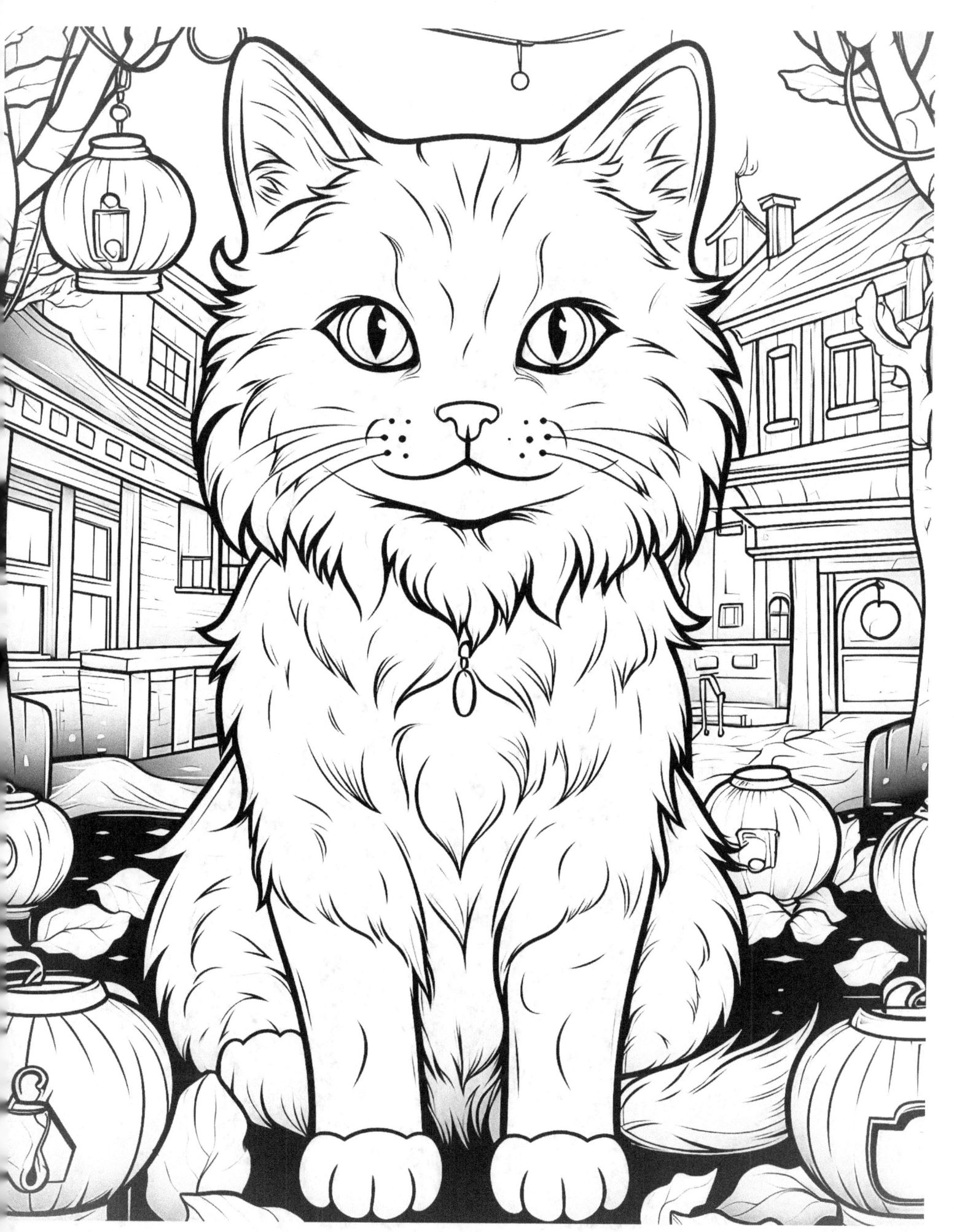

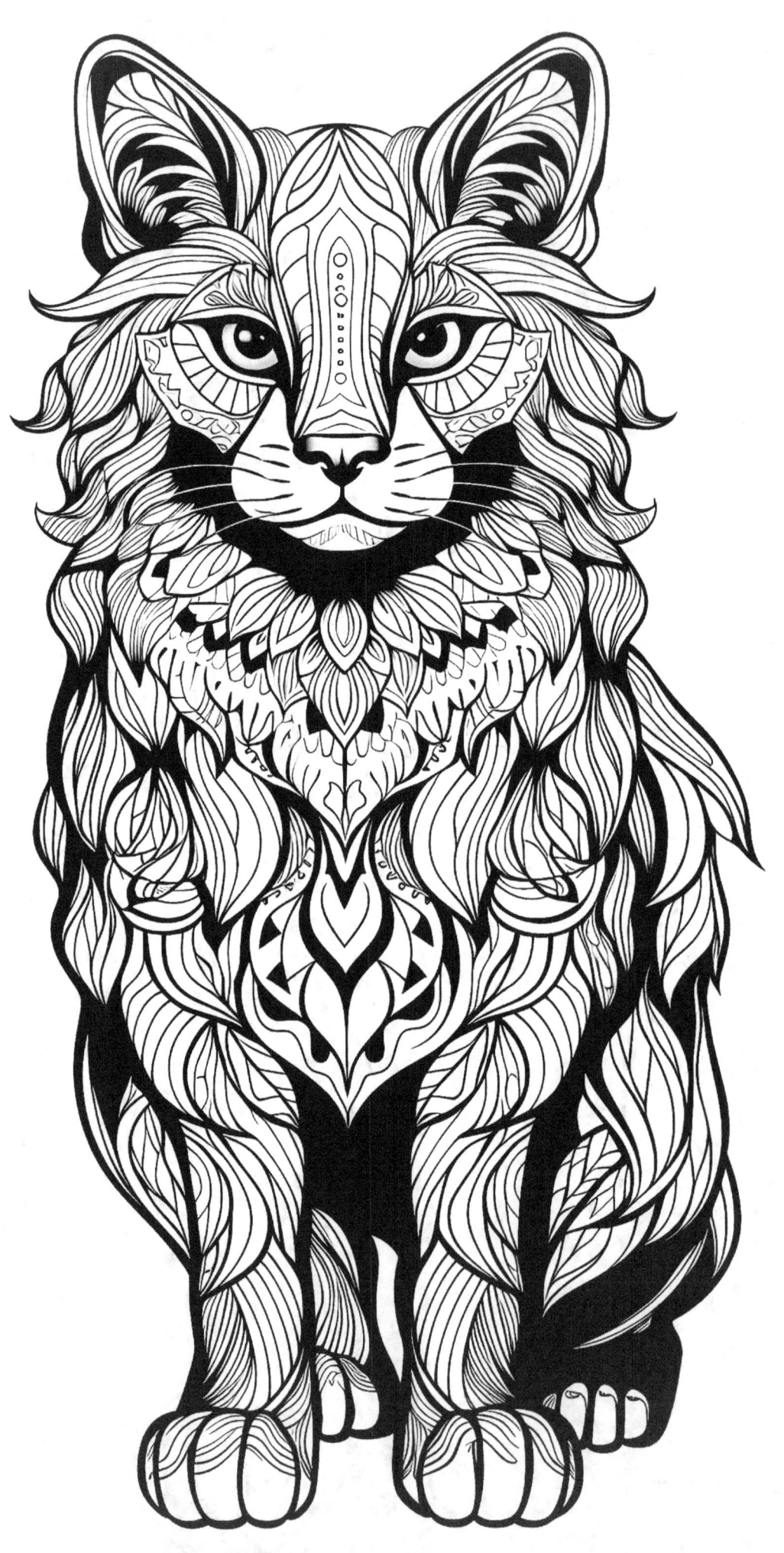